Infantry Weapons of the World

CHRISTOPHER F FOSS
& T J GANDER

LONDON

IAN ALLAN LTD

First published 1977

ISBN 07110 0734 9

Published by Ian Allan Ltd, Shepperton, Surrey and printed and bound in the United Kingdom by R J Acford Ltd, Industrial Estate, Chichester, Sussex.

Contents

Abbreviations

AA	Anti-Aircraft
AFV	Armoured Fighting Vehicle
AR	Assault Rifle
AT	Anti-Tank
ATGW	Anti-Tank Guided Weapon
cm	Centimetre(s)
FGR	Federal German Republic
FN	Fabrique Nationale (Belgium)
gr	Gramme(s)
GPMG	General Purpose Machine Gun
HE	High Explosive
HEAT	High Explosive Anti-Tank
HMG	Heavy Machine Gun
IMI	Israel Military Industries
kg	Kilogram(s)
LAR	Light Assault Rifle
LHS	Left Hand Side
LMG	Light Machine Gun
m	Metre(s)
mm	Millimetre(s)
m/s	Metres a Second
m/v	Muzzle Velocity
MG	Machine Gun
MMG	Medium Machine Gun
NATO	North Atlantic Treaty Organisation
PRC	Peoples' Republic of China
RHS	Right Hand Side
RR	Recoilless Rifle
rpm	Rounds Per Minute
SMG	Sub-Machine Gun
TAVR	Territorial Army Volunteer Reserve (UK)
UK	United Kingdom
USA	United States of America

Acknowledgements

The authors would like to thank the following companies and individuals for their most valuable assistance in the preparation of this book.

Aerojet Ordnance and Manufacturing Company (USA)
Airborne Forces Museum (Aldershot, England)
Argentine Ministry of Defence
Armalite Incorporated (USA)
Austrian Army
Beretta (Italy)
Breda (Italy)
Carl Walther (Germany)
CETME (Spain)
Colt Industries (USA)
Esperanza Company (Spain)
FFV (Sweden)
Finnish Army
FN (Belgium)
French Army
German Army
Heckler and Koch GmbH (Germany)
Irish Army
Israel Military Industries
Ministry of Defence (Army), United Kingdom
Norwegian Army
Peter Chamberlain
Rheinmetall GmbH (Germany)
Soltam Limited (Israel)
Sterling Armament Company (Great Britain)
Steyr-Daimler-Puch AG (Austria)
Sturm, Ruger and Company Incorporated (USA)
Swiss Industrial Group
Thomson-Brandt (France)
United Kingdom Land Forces
United States Army
United States Marine Corps

Glossary

Ammunition	Term for the complete round needed to fire a gun.
Automatic	A weapon that will fire, reload and fire until prevented from doing so by an external mechanism. Often used to describe a semi-automatic pistol.
Barrel	A steel tube in a gun along which the bullet is fired.
Bolt	A metal device that holds the round in the chamber ready for firing. May be mechanically or physically locked or free to move as in a blowback mechanism.
Blowback	General term used to describe the action of many automatic weapons when an unlocked bolt is returned to the rear by the explosion of the cartridge propellant. Locking is usually effected by the mass of the breechblock.
Breech	Rear face of the barrel.
Breechblock	Part of an action that holds or locks the round into the chamber for firing and moves back for ejection of the spent cartridge and loading of the next round.
Bullet	The projectile fired from a small-arm.
Butt/Butt stock	On a shoulder arm the part of the weapon against the firer's shoulder. On a hand gun the part of the gun held in the hand.
Calibre/Caliber	Internal dimension of the barrel measured from land to land.
Carbine	Short rifle.
Cartridge	A complete round of fixed ammunition.
Chamber	Part of the barrel that holds the cartridge ready for firing.
Change lever	Lever usually near the trigger that selects mode of fire. Usually has three positions — automatic, single shot, safe. Sometimes called selector lever or catch.
Cocking	The action of mechanically or manually preparing a weapon's mechanism ready for firing.
Cocking handle	The handle or lever used to cock a weapon.
Compensator	A muzzle attachment used to direct some portion of the gases escaping from the muzzle upwards to counteract a weapon's tendency to rise when fired.
Cylinder	The part of a revolver used to hold rounds ready for firing.
Ejector	Part of a gun mechanism that forces the spent cartridge case out of the gun. Usually a fixed projection.
Extractor	Part of a gun mechanism, usually on a bolt or breechblock that withdraws the cartridge case from the chamber.
Firing pin	Part of the firing mechanism that actually strikes the primer to fire the gun. May be fixed or mechanically operated, and is usually on the bolt, breechblock or frame.
Flash hider	Device fixed to the muzzle to hide the flash produced when firing. Sometimes known as a flash suppressor.
Frame	Part of a revolver that carries the cylinder and barrel. May be fixed or hinged.
Hammer	Swinging part of a firing mechanism which may hit the primer for firing, or deliver the force via a firing pin. Usually fitted to revolvers, and may be internal or external.
Handgun	Term used to denote a firearm that can be held in one hand.
Jacket	Metal covering of a bullet.
Kick	Recoil forces felt by the firer of a weapon.
Land	Raised portion of rifling.
Magazine	Device used on small arms to hold rounds ready for loading and firing. May be either box type or drum.
Mainspring	Internal spring used to drive forward a bolt or breechblock.
Muzzle velocity	Speed of a bullet as it leaves the muzzle. Sometimes referred to as V_0.
Pistol	Term used to signify a handgun in which the chamber is permanently aligned with the barrel. This includes revolvers and some automatic pistols but the term is now usually used to cover any form of handgun.
Primer	A small charge in the base of a cartridge which fires the main propellant. On most small arms this is done mechanically but some weapons use electricity.

Glossary (cont.)

Propellant	The charge inside a cartridge that propels the bullet.
Range	The distance to which a bullet can be fired. Usually defined as maximum practical which is the range at which the bullet will still have a useful striking power.
Rate of fire	Number of rounds fired per minute. The *Cyclic* rate is that possible in one minute if an uninterrupted supply of ammunition is maintained. The *practical* rate includes the time lost for changing magazines, etc.
Receiver	Part of weapon containing the bolt/breechblock and mainspring, sometimes known as the body.
Revolver	Type of handgun that holds available rounds in a cylinder.
Rifle	General term used to denote a small-arm with a long rifled barrel that usually fires single shots only.
Rifling	Grooves cut inside a barrel to impart stabilising spin to a bullet.
Round	General term used to denote cartridge.
Safety/Safety catch	Mechanical or manually applied device to prevent a weapon firing.
Sear	Lever between the trigger and firing pin or hammer to give controlled leverage to firing mechanism.
Semi-automatic	Term applied to small-arm that fires once, ejects spent case reloads but does not fire again until the trigger is pressed.
Sidearm	Small-arms that can be carried on a belt and fired from one hand. Was used to denote pistols only but now also includes small submachine guns.
Sights	Devices used to aim a weapon accurately. Divided into fore and rear sights. The foresight is usually a fixed metal post or spline, while the rear sight is usually at the rear of the weapon and may incorporate many refinements such as a ramp or rising frame to accommodate increases in range or wind velocity. The simplest rearsight on a pistol is usually a simple notch to be aligned with the foresight. Some weapons use telescopic or other optical sights. A flipsight is a folding rearsight which can be 'flipped up' for use.
Singlepoint	A new form of weapon sight that projects a white spot in a tube over a small-arm to visual infinity. Aligning the white spot (while both the firer's eyes are open) will accurately aim the weapon.
Slide	An external breechblock, usually found on semi-automatic pistols.
Small-arm	General term that is usually used to refer to a weapon that can be carried by one man.
Stock	Part of a small-arm held by the firer and used to aim the weapon. Usually of wood but plastic and metal are now often used.
Submachine gun	Automatic weapon, firing pistol ammunition, with a short barrel carried and used by one man.
Trigger	Lever operated manually to fire a weapon.

Introduction

Infantry Weapons of the World contains full details of all the important infantry weapons in current use throughout the world. In addition some of the many weapons that are still under development have been included to complete the picture.

Weapons covered include pistols, sub-machine guns, rifles, light, medium and heavy machine guns, light mortars and light anti-tank weapons. Medium mortars (ie mortars of 81 mm and over) and heavy recoilless weapons such as the Wombat and M40 are full covered in the companion volume *Artillery of the World*. Anti-tank missiles such as HOT, TOW, MILAN and SWINGFIRE are covered in another Companion Volume *Missiles of the World*.

Not all pistols and rifles are covered as many commercial weapons are used by para-military units. Shotguns have also been excluded although these are used by some countries for guerrilla and internal security operations as they are in most cases standard commercial weapons. It will be appreciated that some very old weapons have been excluded due to lack of space as have a number of weapons of local manufacture.

In the 1950's NATO adopted the 7.62mm round as its standard round for both rifles and light machine guns. In the 1960's however the United States adopted a 5.56mm rifle round. Initially this was only issued to troops in Vietnam whilst European-based troops still retained the 7.62mm M14 rifle. Several years ago all United States Army units were equipped with the 5.56mm M16 rifle. Thus both 5.56mm and 7.62mm weapons are in service in the Central Region. The situation on the flanks of NATO is also un-standard as some countries still have American, British and German rifles and weapons of World War 2 vintage in front line use.

Belgium, France and Germany have all developed 5.56mm weapons and Britain is known to be working on a new range of small arms. Israel, Italy, Sweden and Switzerland have all developed 5.56mm weapons and the Galil Assault Rifle is already in service with the Israel Army and will soon be available for export.

Whilst the standard 5.56mm round is satisfactory for the rifle, doubts have been expressed about its suitability for use in light machine guns as the round lacks range and penetration. With this in mind FN have developed the 5.56mm Minimi machine gun which fires a heavier 5.56mm round than the normal 5.56mm rifle.

The Warsaw Pact still uses the 7.62mm round but they are known to be working on a new range of weapons in 5.56mm calibre.

Many countries in NATO are now developing new lightweight anti-tank weapons for the use of the infantry which will be more portable and effective than current weapons in use. Within NATO there appear, however, to be far too many projects under way especially in the small arms and light anti-tank weapons field. It is clear that in these days of falling defence budgets and increasing costs, there must be more standardisation within the Alliance if it is to have the best weapons in adequate numbers in the future.

The authors would like to thank the many governments, individuals and manufacturers who have provided material for this book. Additional material, including photographs, should be forwarded to *Infantry Weapons of the World,* Ian Allan Limited, Terminal House, Shepperton, TW17 8AS, England.

Christopher F Foss
T J Gander

9mm PA3-DM Sub-Machine Gun

Argentina

Calibre: 9mm
Length with Fixed Butt: 70cm
Length with Wire Butt: 69.3cm
Length with Wire Butt Retracted: 52.3cm
Weight with Fixed Butt-Loaded: 3.9kg
Weight with Wire Butt-Loaded: 3.95kg
Magazine Capacity: 25 rounds
Barrel Length: 29cm
Muzzle Velocity: 400m/s
Maximum Effective Range: 200m
Rate of Fire: 650rpm(cyclic)

This weapon has been influenced in the design stage by the Israeli Uzi SMG and employs a similar pistol-grip magazine and a similar bolt extending over the barrel. It can be used with either a plastic butt or a sliding wire butt. Like most modern SMG's it can be used to fire grenades. It is in service with the Argentinian Army.

Below: *The 9mm PA3-DM Sub-Machine Gun with butt extended.*

9mm F1 Sub-Machine Gun

Australia

Calibre: 9mm
Length: **71.4cm**
Length of Barrel: 20.3cm
Weight Loaded: 4.47kg
Weight Empty: 3.26kg
Magazine Capacity: 34 rounds
Muzzle Velocity: 366m/s
Maximum Effective Range: 200m
Rate of Fire: 600rpm(cyclic)
120rpm(practical)

The F1 was designed in 1959–1961 and went into production in 1962 to replace the Owen and Austen SMG's then in service. It is a conventional blow-back weapon with little of note apart from the vertically mounted curved magazine. When used in action in Vietnam its low-powered round was considered unsuitable and the type was replaced in front-line service with the American AR-15.

Below: *The 9mm F1 Sub-Machine Gun.*

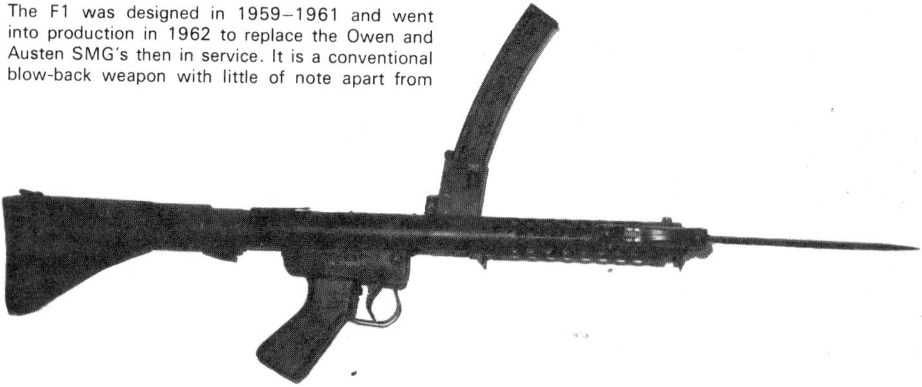

7.62mm L2A1 Heavy Barrelled Rifle

Australia

Calibre: 7.62mm
Length: 113.7cm
Length of Barrel: 53.3cm
Weight: 6.9kg
Magazine Capacity: 30 rounds
Muzzle Velocity: 838m/s
Range: 800m
Rate of Fire: 650/700rpm(cyclic)
40rpm(single shots)

The 7.62mm L1A1 is the standard rifle of the Australian Army, and has been built under licence from FN at the small arms factory at Lithgow, New South Wales. A special shortened model was provided for use in New Guinea.

The L2A1 is a heavy barrelled version of the L1A1 and is used by non-infantry units for fire support, the infantry units use the 7.62mm Bren and the M60 for this role.

The L2A1 is provided with a bipod. Its foresight is of the blade type and the rear sight of the aperture type. In concept the L2A1 is similar to the Belgian 7.62mm FN LAR and the Canadian C2/C2A1 heavy barrelled rifle.

.22 AM 180 Sub-Machine Gun

Austria/United States

Calibre: .22
Length: 90cm
64.5cm(without stock)
Length of Barrel: 42.5cm
Weight: 4.5kg(loaded)
3.9kg(empty)

Below: *Top the AM 180 with Laser Lok sight, center the standard AM 180, and below a new AM 180 with stock removed and a foregrip fitted.*

Magazine Capacity: 177 rounds
Range: 160m(maximum)
Rate of Fire: 1600rpm(cyclic)

The AM 180 has been developed by the American International Corporation of Salt Lake City, Utah, and is manufactured in Austria by the Voere Company. Over 1 000 have been sold, most of which have gone to police forces in the United States and elsewhere.

It fires from the open bolt using the blowback principle. The user can select either full automatic or semi-automatic and the weapon fires the standard .22 long rifle round with a m/v of 412m/s.

The forestock is of a durable plastic construction as is the removable stock. The foresight is of the protected blade type and the rear sight is of the peep type and is adjustable in both the vertical and horizontal plane. According to the manufacturer, the main advantages of the AM 180 are that muzzle blast, barrel climb and barrel rotation are virtually non-existant. During trials, all 177 rounds were fired into a 7.5cm circle at a range of 18m.

A Laser Lok sight is also available for this weapon and this is mounted under the barrel. This provides pinpoint accuracy in dim light or night conditions by emitting a red dot that is about 7cm in diameter at 160m and indicates the point of impact.

The AM 180 is also available in a short barrel version with a folding shoulder stock.

Below: *The AM 180 stripped down showing all components.*

Steyr-Daimler-Puch 9mm MPi 69 SMG — Austria

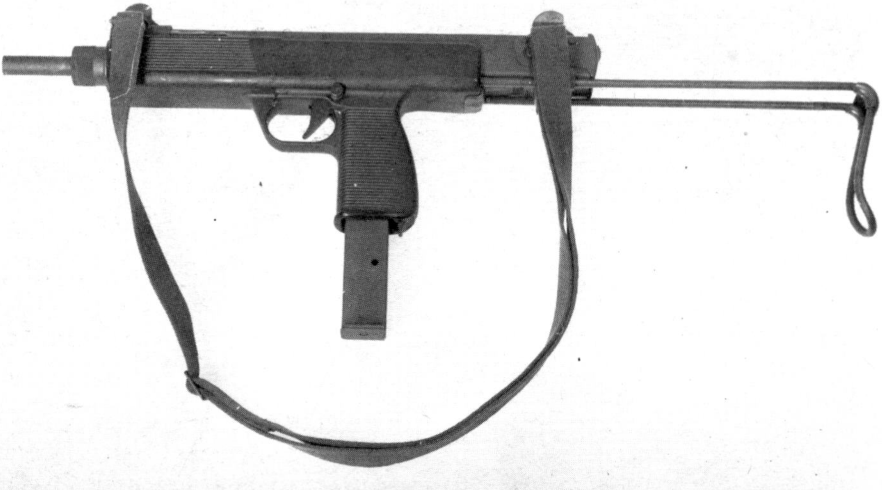

Calibre: 9mm
Length—Butt Extended: 67.3cm
Length—Butt Retracted: 47cm
Length of Barrel: 26cm
Weight Loaded: 3.52kg
Magazine Capacity: 25 rounds
Muzzle Velocity: 381m/s
Maximum Effective Range: 200m
Rate of Fire: 400rpm(cyclic)

Despite the outward similarities with the Israeli Uzi SMG, the MPi 69 has many differences not the least of which is the unusual trigger mechanism. Instead of the usual two-position selector, the MPi 69 uses a dual-pressure trigger. A short squeeze will give single shots, while a definite pull-back will give full automatic fire. The cocking method is also unusual as it uses a backward pull on the sling which has to be held at right angles to the gun for the purpose. As well as the usual fixed sights, (two leaves at either 100 or 200m), a Singlepoint sight can be fitted as standard. This weapon is in service with the Austrian Army and has been offered to the Saudi-Arabian Forces.

Bottom left: *The Steyr-Daimler-Puch 9mm MPi 69 Sub-Machine Gun.*

7.62mm SSG 69 Rifle

Austria

Calibre: 7.62mm
Length: 113cm
Length of Barrel: 65cm
Weight: 4.5kg(with sight but without ammunition)
Magazine Capacity: 5 rounds
Muzzle Velocity: 860m/s
Range: 800m

The SSG 69 (Scharfschuetzengewehr 69) is the standard sniping rifle of the Austrian Army and is built by Steyr-Daimler-Puch. It fires a 7.62mm × 51 cartridge and this weapon is also available commercially.

It is bolt-operated and fed from a five-round rotating spool magazine.

Its normal sights are a blade foresight and a V-type back sight. Army models retain these but also have a Kahles Helia 6S2 telescopic sight with a magnification of × 6 which is graduated up to 800m. If required, an infra-red or image-intensifier sight can be fitted in place of the telescopic sight.

Below: *7.62mm SSG 69 Sniper's Rifle.*

9mm Browning HP Pistol — Belgium

Calibre: 9mm
Length: 196mm
Length of Barrel: 112mm
Weight Loaded: 1.01kg
Magazine Capacity: 13 rounds
Muzzle Velocity: 354m/s
Maximum Effective Range: 45m

Since this pistol was introduced into production in 1935 (it was designed in 1925), it has become one of the most widely used of all automatic pistols. It was first produced in Belgium (as the GP-Grand Puissance) but since then has been produced in many other countries, the most important of which has been Canada where the type has been produced for military and civil use as the 'High Power'. The HP can be found with both fixed and ramp rear-sights and some versions have provision for a butt stock. There are numerous variations and copies. The HP is in service with the British Army as the standard hand weapon, and is used by many other armed forces. The type is still in widespread use in the Far East where many 'pirate' copies from a variety of sources remain in use. It is also built in Argentina and the Indonesians built it as the Pindad.

Above: *the 9mm Browning HP Pistol.*

Mitraillette Vigneron 9mm M2 — Belgium

Calibre: 9mm
Length—Butt Extended: 88.6cm
Length—Butt Retracted: 70.6cm
Length of Barrel: 30.5cm
Weight Loaded: 3.69kg
Magazine Capacity: 32 rounds
Muzzle Velocity: 381m/s
Maximum Effective Range: 200m
Rate of Fire: 620rpm(cyclic)

Designed by Colonel Vigneron, the M2 was adopted by the Belgian Army in 1953. Some remain in use in the Congo Republics and Luxembourg as well as with the Belgian Army.

Right: *The Mitraillette Vigneron 9mm M2 Sub-Machine Gun.*

5.56mm FN CAL Rifle

Belgium

Calibre: 5.56mm
Length: 98cm
115.3cm(with bayonet)
Length of Barrel: 48.25cm
Weight: 3.3kg(without magazine)
.55kg(loaded 30-round steel magazine)
.4kg(loaded 20-round steel magazine)
Magazine Capacity: 20 or 30 rounds
Muzzle Velocity: 895m/s
Maximum Effective Range: 400m
Rate of Fire: 650—700rpm(cyclic)
120rpm(automatic)
60rpm(single shots)

The 5.56mm FN CAL(Carabine Automatique Légère) was developed in the early 1960's and was one of the first European rifles to be built in 5.56mm calibre. Two models are available, one with a conventional stock and the other with a folding metal stock. To date neither has been placed in production.

The weapon is gas-operated and the method of locking is the rotating-bolt method. The firer can select either full automatic, three round bursts or single shots. Both 20- and 30-round magazines are available. The front sight is of the cylindrical post type and the rear sight is of the flip aperture type being graduated for 250 and 400m.

The CAL has three safety features:

1. Manual. The change lever axis acts directly on the trigger.
2. The safety sear frees the hammer only after the locking has taken place.
3. The firing pin, without spring, is held backward until the bolt is in the locking position.

The following accessories are available—removable bipod, bayonet and a blank firing device.

Below: *The FN 5.56mm CAL Rifle.*

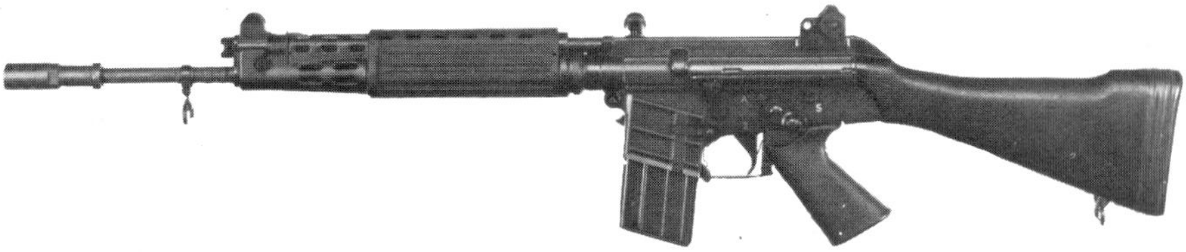

7.62mm FN FAL Rifle

Belgium

Calibre: 7.62mm
Length: 200cm
Length of Barrel: 53.3cm
Weight Empty: 4.31kg
Weight Loaded: 5.06kg
Magazine Capacity: 20 rounds
Muzzle Velocity: 823m/s
Maximum Effective Range: 600m
Rate of Fire: 650—700rpm(cyclic)
120rpm(auto)
60rpm(single shot)

Design work on an automatic rifle in Belgium began before WW2 and in 1949 a .280 'Bull-pup' design was produced after experiments with a 7.92mm 'kurz' round model. With the demise of the .280 round the design was altered to a conventional layout and the result became known as the FN Fusil Automatique Légère, or FAL. In this form it became an enormous export success and a list of user countries is below. Manufacturing licences were taken up by several countries, one of the most important of which is the United Kingdom where the type was produced as the L1A1 with the automatic feature removed. There are many variations on the basic FAL theme as some models are fitted with folding frame butts (LAR) and some versions are produced with heavy barrels and bipods to enable the weapon to be used as a LMG (eg, the Australian L2A1 and the Canadian Rifle, Automatic, FN C2A1). The FAL has a gas-operated mechanism, can be used to fire grenades, and a variety of accessories can be fitted.

User Nations—those marked with a * have manufacturing licences.

FN FAL Argentina*, Austria*, Belgium*, Burundi Cambodia, Chile, Cuba, Dominica, Dubai, Ecuador, Eire, Ghana, India*, Indonesia, Israel*, Kuwait, Liberia, Libya, Luxemburg, Malawi, Morocco, Mozambique, Netherlands, Norway*, Paraguay, Peru, Portugal, South Africa, West Germany.
L1A1 Australia*, Barbados, Canada*, Gambia, Guyana, Malaysia, Muscat, New Zealand, Singapore, United Kingdom*

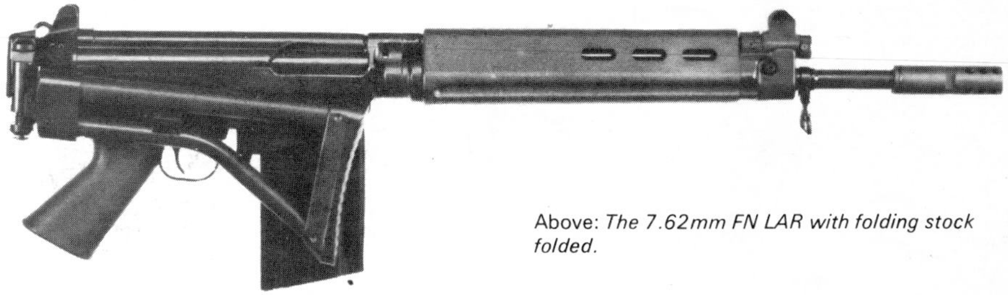

Above: *The 7.62mm FN LAR with folding stock folded.*

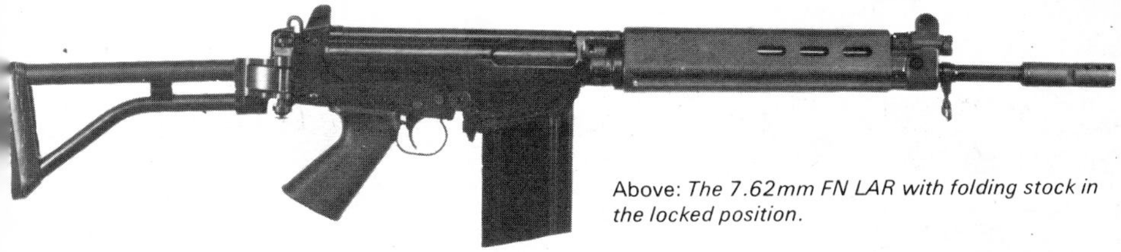

Above: *The 7.62mm FN LAR with folding stock in the locked position.*

Left: *The 7.62mm FN FAL Rifle being used by a British soldier.*

Below: *The 7.62mm FN FAL with bipod, heavy barrel and telescopic sights.*

5.56mm FN Minimi Machine Gun

Belgium

Calibre: 5.56mm
Length: 100cm
Length of Barrel: 46.8cm
Weight: 8.8kg(with 200 rounds)
6.5kg(with bipod but without magazine)
6.2kg(without magazine or ammunition)
Magazine Capacity: 100 or 200 rounds
Muzzle Velocity: 935m/s
Effective Range: 500m
Rate of Fire: 750/1 000rpm

The Minimi is the latest weapon to come from the FN stable. It has been designed to fire 5.56mm ammunition with a projectile weighing 3.6 grammes, a 4gramme round has however been specially developed for the Minimi and this will penetrate a steel helmet at a range of 800m. A tracer round with a m/v of 780m/s is under development. At a range of 400m the 4gramme round has a velocity of 507m/s and at 600m it is 310m/s.

The MG is gas-operated and the gas comes from the forward part of the barrel. The gas regulator has three positions—normal, emergency and grenade launching. The firer can select either full automatic fire or controlled bursts, ie 3–6 rounds. The barrel can be quickly replaced.

The weapon is available with a fixed stock, folding stock or without a stock for turret applications. A carrying handle is provided and the bipod can be folded up underneath the barrel if required. A tripod weighing 6kg is under development.

The ammunition is held together by disintegrating links and magazines holding 100 or 200 rounds are available; these are attached to the weapon.

Below: *The FN 5.56mm Minimi Machine Gun without magazine.*

7.62mm FN MAG

Belgium

Calibre: 6.5 and 7.62mm
Length: 125.5cm
Length of Barrel: 54.5cm
Weight with Bipod: 10.85kg
Weight Minus Butt and Bipod: 10.1kg
Weight of Tripod: 10.5kg
Type of Feed: 50-round link belts
Continuous disintegrating link belts
Muzzle Velocity: 840m/s
Maximum Effective Range: 1 200m
Rate of Fire: 600-1 000rpm(cyclic)
250rpm(automatic)

The FN MAG (Mitrailleuse à Gaz) was designed at Herstal during the early 1950s and soon became an export success to the extent that it is now in use all over the world. The United Kingdom took up a manufacturing licence and introduced some changes to produce the L7A1 series (cf.). The FN MAG can be used either on a bipod or on a tripod for the extended fire role, for which role the quick barrel change feature is useful.

Above: *The 7.62mm FN MAG Machine Gun with bipod.*

Below: *The 7.62mm FN MAG Machine Gun with tripod.*

RL-100 Anti-Tank Weapon

Belgium

Calibre: 101mm
Weight: 12.9kg
Length: 188.5cm (deployed)
102cm(folded)
Range: 400m
Crew: 1

The RL-100 was designed and built by Mecar SA of Belgium. It is still used by the Belgian Army but is no longer in production.

A bipod is provided at the muzzle end of the weapon and it can be folded for easy transportation. It fires a HEAT round which weighs 2.75kg, has a muzzle velocity of 195m/s and will penetrate 400mm of armour.

Above: *The RL-100 Anti-Tank Weapon.*

RL-83 (Blindicide) Anti-Tank Weapon

Belgium

Calibre: 83mm
Weight: 8.4kg(with 900m sight)
Length: 170cm(in action)
92cm(folded)
Range: 900m(maximum)
400m(effective)
Crew: 1

The RL-83 was designed and built by Mecar SA of Belgium. It is still used by the Belgian Army but is no longer in production.

It can be fired from a bipod which is mounted at the forward part of the barrel or from the shoulder. A variety of rounds have been developed for the weapon including HEAT, Illuminating, smoke, incendiary and anti-personnel.
The HEAT projectile has a m/v of 100m/s.
Three types of sight are available:
1. Standard metal sight for targets up to 400m.
2. Optical sight with same range as above.
3. Auxiliary sight to extend the range to 900m.

Below: *The RL-83 Blindicide Anti-Tank Weapon.*

Weapons in Service with the People's Republic of China

The People's Republic of China armed forces employ a large range of infantry weapons many of which are locally made copies of weapons in service in the Soviet Bloc Armies. To prevent repetition a listing has been made of most of these types.

Pistols
7.62mm Type 51 (Copy of Tokarev TT33)
7.62mm Type 54 (Copy of Tokarev TT33)
9mm Type 59 (Copy of Makarov)

Sub-Machine Guns
7.62mm Type 50 (Copy of PPSh-41)
7.62mm Type 43 (Copy of PPS-43)

Rifles
7.62mm Type 53 Carbine (Copy of Model 1944 Carbine)
7.62mm Type 56 S.A. Carbine (Copy of SKS)
7.62mm Type 56 Assault Rifle (Copy of AK-47)
7.62mm Type 56-1 Assault Rifle (Copy of AK-47 with folding stock)

Light Machine Guns
7.62mm Type 53 (Copy of DPM)
7.62mm Type 56 (Copy of RPD)
7.62mm Type 58 (Copy of RP-46)

Medium Machine Gun
7.62mm Type 57 (Copy of SGM)

Heavy Machine Gun
12.7mm Type 54 (Copy of Model 38/46)

Light Mortar
60mm Type 31 (Copy of American Mortar 60mm M2)
60mm Type 63 (Revised Type 31)

Anti-Tank Weapons
87mm Type 51 (Copy of American 3.5 inch Rocket Launcher M20)
57mm RR Type 36 (Copy of American M18 Recoilless Rifle)
40mm A/T Grenade Launcher Type 56 (Copy of Soviet RPG-2 Weapon)
40mm A/T Grenade Launcher Type 69 (Copy of Soviet RPG-7 Weapon)

7.65mm Type 64 Silenced Pistol China(PRC)

Calibre: 7.65mm
Length: 33cm
Length of Barrel: 12.4cm
Weight: 1.27kg
Magazine Capacity: 8 rounds or single shot
Muzzle Velocity: 274m/s
Maximum Range: 35m

This unusual weapon has been developed purely as a close-range silent assassination weapon and it fires a unique 7.65mm × 17 rimless round. Although it has an automatic mechanism, it would seem that it is intended primarily as a hand-operated single-shot weapon.

7.62mm Type 64 Silenced Sub-Machine Gun China(PRC)

Calibre: 7.62mm
Length—Stock Open: 84.3cm
Length—Stock Folded: 63.5cm
Length of Barrel: 24.4cm
Weight Empty: 3.4kg
Magazine Capacity: 30 rounds
Muzzle Velocity: 513m/s
Maximum Effective Range: 135m
Rate of Fire: 1 315rpm(cyclic)

The Type 64 has a rather varied design origin as it seems to be made up of a number of design features from other weapons. For example, the trigger mechanism has been copied from that of the Bren Gun while the bolt action is derived from the Russian PPS-43. The silencer is not completely effective but it has the virtue of hiding any flash while at the same time masking much of the muzzle blast noise. This weapon is in service with the Chinese armed forces and has seen action in Vietnam.

7.62mm Type 68 Rifle

China(PRC)

Calibre: 7.62mm
Length: 102.9cm
Length of Barrel: 52.1cm
Weight: 3.49kg
Magazine Capacity: 15 or 30 rounds
Muzzle Velocity: 730m/s
Maximum Effective Range—Single: 400m
Maximum Effective Range—Auto: 200m
Rate of Fire: 750rpm(cyclic)
85rpm(auto)
40rpm(single)

The Type 68 at first sight is similar to the Russian AK-47 but it differs in some respects. It has a longer barrel and uses a different trigger mechanism. The usual magazine used has a 15-round capacity but the Type 56 (AK-47) magazine can also be fitted. Early versions had a receiver machined from solid metal but later versions have steel pressings.

7.62mm Type 67 Light Machine Gun

China(PRC)

Calibre: 7.62mm
Length: 114.3cm
Length of Barrel: 59.7cm
Weight: 8.8kg
Type of Feed: 100-round link belt
Muzzle Velocity: 835m/s
Maximum Effective Range: 800m
Rate of Fire: 650rpm(cyclic)
150rpm(automatic)

This weapon was designed to replace the large and varied number of types of machine gun in service in Communist China. It features a number of design features taken from existing designs and is gas-operated. It has been in action in Vietnam.

7.62mm Vzor Pistol (Vz52)

Czechoslovakia

Calibre: 7.62mm
Length: 21cm
Length of Barrel: 12cm
Weight: 1.045kg(with loaded 8-round magazine)
.965kg(with empty 8-round magazine)
.887kg(without magazine)
Magazine Capacity: 8 rounds
Range: 50m

The Vz52 is an eight-shot, semi-automatic, short recoil-operated, magazine-fed weapon. It has been replaced to some extent by the Vz61(Skorpion) Machine Pistol.

The Vz52 fires the 7.62 × 25mm cartridge with a m/v of 492m/s. It is issued complete with a holster and a cleaning rod. Its foresight is of the blade type and its rearsight is of the square notch type. The ejection port is on the RHS and the safety catch is on the LHS. The Vz50 is a 7.65mm pistol that is used by the Czechoslovakian Police.

Bottom left: *The 7.62mm Vzor(Vz52) Pistol.*

7.65mm M-61 Skorpion Machine Pistol (Vzor 61) Czechoslovakia

Calibre: 7.65mm
Length: 5.13cm(with stock extended)
2.69cm(weapon only)
Length of Barrel: 11.2cm
Weight: 1.55kg(with 20-round magazine)
1.45kg(with 10-round magazine)
1.29kg(without magazine)
Magazine Capacity: 10- or 20-round magazine
Range: 100/200m(with stock, semi-automatic)
50m(with stock, automatic)
Rate of Fire: 750rpm(cyclic)

The Vzor 61 is a blowback operated weapon that is capable of both full automatic or semi-automatic fire. The weapon can be used as a pistol or with its stock as a light SMG. The metal stock folds through 180° when not required. The Vzor fires the standard 7.65mm Browning commercial cartridge with a m/v of 317m/s. When being used on automatic its practical rate of fire is 100rpm and when on semi-automatic its practical rate of fire is 35rpm. The selector is on the LHS and has the marking 20 for automatic fire and 1 for single shots as well as for safe. If required, it can be fitted with a bayonet, silencer and luminous sights for use at night. The foresight is of the cylindrical post type and the rearsight is of the flip type with two settings, one for 75m and the other for 150m. Both hip and shoulder holsters are available for the VZOR 61.

Below: *The 7.65mm M-61 Skorpion Machine Pistol.*

9mm M23 and M25 Sub-Machine Guns(Vzor 23 and Vzor 25)

Czechoslovakia

Calibre: 9mm
Length: 68.6cm(stock extended)
44.5cm(stock folded)
Length of Barrel: 28.4cm
Weight: 4.1kg(with loaded 40-round magazine)
4.06kg(with loaded 24-round magazine)
3.68kg(with empty 40-round magazine)
3.64kg(with empty 24-round magazine)
3.4kg(without magazine)
Magazine Capacity: 24 or 40 rounds
Range: 150m(Semi-automatic)
100m(automatic)
Rate of Fire: 650rpm(cyclic)
50rpm(semi-automatic)
80/100rpm(automatic)

Above data relates to the Vzor 25

These weapons entered service with the Czechoslovakian Army after World War 2, and remained until they were replaced by the similar M24 and M25 weapons. These are chambered for 7.62mm cartridges. The M23 has a fixed wooden stock and the M25 a folding metal stock. They both fire the 9 × 19mm parabellum cartridge with a m/v of 450m/s and their box magazines go straight up through the handle. They can be fired either semi-automatic or full automatic; the type of fire is controlled by the amount of pressure that is applied to the trigger. An unusual feature is that the bolt is hollow and overrides the barrel, this permits the use of a longer barrel for better ballistic performance without lengthening the weapon itself.

Below: *The 9mm M23 Sub-Machine Gun with fixed wooden stock.*
Bottom: *The 9mm M25 Sub-Machine Gun with folding metal stock.*

7.62mm M24 and M26 Sub-Machine Guns(Vzor 24 and Vzor 26)

Czechoslovakia

Calibre: 7.62mm
Length: 68.5cm
Length of Barrel: 28.5cm
Weight: 3.98kg(with loaded 32-round magazine)
3.64kg(with 32-round magazine empty)
3.38kg(with no magazine)
Magazine Capacity: 32 rounds
Range: 150m(semi-automatic)
100m (automatic)
Rate of Fire: 650rpm(cyclic)
50rpm(semi-automatic)
80/100rpm(automatic)

This is basically the M23 and M25 9mm sub-machine guns chambered to fire the 7.62mm × 25P round with a m/v of 550m/s. Apart from the change in calibre they have a heavier bolt and a new magazine to take the longer 7.62mm round. They are distinguishable from the earlier weapons as their magazines have a forward pitch. The M24 has a wooden stock and the M26 a folding metal stock. Like the earlier weapons, they are of rugged, simple construction, much use being made of stamped parts.

7.62mm Vzor 58 Assault Rifle (Vz58P or Vz58V)

Czechoslovakia

Calibre: 7.62mm
Length: 100cm(with bayonet)
84.5cm(rifle only)
65cm(Vz58V with stock folded)
Length of Barrel: 39cm
Weight: 3.77kg(loaded with bayonet)
3.59kg(loaded without bayonet)
3.28kg(with empty magazine and bayonet)
3.1kg(with empty magazine)
2.91kg(without magazine)
.68kg(loaded magazine)
.19kg(empty magazine)
.18kg(bayonet)
Magazine Capacity: 30 rounds
Range: 300m
Rate of Fire: 800/820rpm(cyclic)
80/100rpm(full automatic)
40rpm(semi-automatic)

Note—above data relates to the Vz58P

The Vzor 58 is the standard assault rifle of the Czechoslovakian Army having been introduced into service in 1958. It is a gas-operated, magazine-fed weapon and although it is similar in appearance to the Soviet AK-47 the design is different. The Vz58 has a swinging-wedge breech-lock and a plunger type hammer whereas the AK-47 has a rotary bolt and a swinging hammer. The Vz58 fires the same 7.62 × 39mm cartridge as the AK-47 although their magazines are not interchangeable.

The Vz58P has the conventional fixed stock and is also known as the M58P. The Vz58V has a folding metal buttstock and is also known as the M58V. There are a number of accessories for this weapon including a sling, bayonet, flash-hider, bipod, sectional cleaning rod, magazine carrier, frontsight wrench and it can also be fitted with the NSP-2 infra-red sight for night operations.

Below: *The 7.62mm Vz58P Assault Rifle with conventional stock.*

7.62mm Semi-Automatic Rifle M52 and M52/57

Czechoslovakia

Calibre: 7.62mm
Length: 120.5cm(with bayonet)
100.5cm(rifle only)
Length of Barrel: 52.3cm
Weight: 4.53kg(with loaded magazine)
4.25kg(with empty magazine)
4.1kg(without magazine)
Magazine Capacity: 10 rounds
Range: 400m

Note—above data relates to the M52/57

The M52 and M52/57 semi-automatic rifles were once the standard equipment of the Czechoslovakian Army. They have now been replaced in front line service by the M58 Assault Rifle.

The M52 and the M52/57 are mechanically identical, both have a permanently attached folding knife bayonet on the LHS. The gas operation of the rifle is somewhat similar to the German World War 2 G51 rifle in that the gas cylinder completely encircles the barrel. The trigger assembly is indentical in operation to that of the American M1 rifle.

The M52 fires the Czechoslovakian 7.62 × 45 cartridge which is also used for the Czech M52 LMG, this has a m/v of 744m/s, practical rate of fire is 25rpm. It is sighted to 1 000m with intervals of 50m. The M52/57 is chambered for the Soviet 7.62 × 39 cartridge with a m/v of 735m/s. It is sighted only to 900m.

Below: *The 7.62mm M52/57 Semi-Automatic Rifle.*

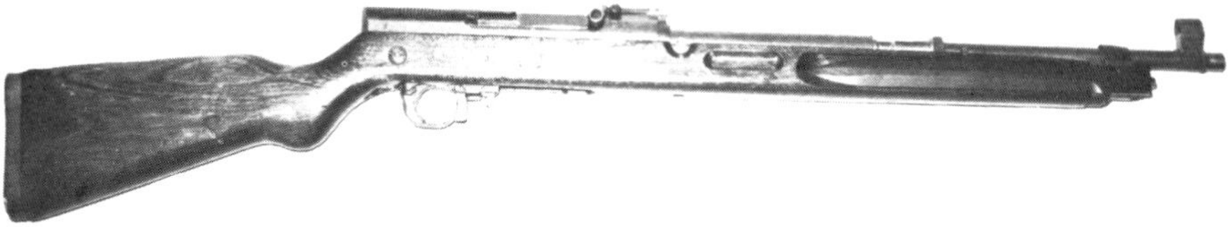

7.62mm Sniper's Rifle M54

Czechoslovakia

Calibre: 7.62mm
Length: 114.8cm
Length of Barrel: 73.2cm
Weight: 4.1kg(with loaded magazine and 'scope)
4kg(with empty magazine and 'scope)
Magazine Capacity: 10 rounds
Range: 1 000m(maximum with 'scope)
800m(maximum combat range)
Rate of Fire: 10rpm

The M54 is similar in appearance to the Soviet M1891/30 rifle but has been cut down to resemble a sporting rifle. It is fitted with a telescopic sight and fires the 7.62 × 54R cartridge with a m/v of 811m/s. It may well have been replaced by the more recent Soviet SVD 7.62mm sniper's rifle.

7.62mm Vzor 59 (Vz59L, Vz59 and Vz59N) General Purpose Machine Gun

Czechoslovakia

	M-59	**M-59L**
Calibre:	7.62mm	7.62mm
Length:	128cm	118.5cm
Length of Barrel:	69.3cm	59.3cm
Weight:	19.5kg	———(on tripod)
	9.37kg	8.77kg(on bipod)
	1.946kg	1.946kg(ammo box with 50 rounds)
	9.15kg	9.15kg(ammo box with 250 rounds)
Range:	1 300m	900m(effective)
	4 800m	4 800m(maximum)
Rate of Fire:	700/850	700/850rpm(cyclic)
	300	150rpm(practical)

The Vz59 is the standard machine gun of the Czechoslovakian Army but is not used by any other Warsaw Pact Forces. It fires the 7.62 × 54R cartridge with a m/v of 760/790m/s. It is also available for export (Vz59N) and the export model fires the 7.62 × 51mm NATO cartridge.

The Vz59L has a short barrel and is provided with a bipod, the 50-round box magazine is attached to the weapon and a carrying handle is provided. The basic Vz59 has the longer and heavier barrel and is normally mounted on a tripod which can also be adopted for the anti-aircraft role very quickly. When used on the tripod it is fed from a 250-round box which is to the right of the weapon.

If required the Vz59 can be fitted with the lighter barrel and mounted on a bipod. It has a pillar type front sight and a V-notch rearsight adjustable from 100m to 2 000m in 100m increments.

The Vz59 and Vz59L can be fitted with a × 4 telescopic sight or the PPN-2 infra-red night sight.

The Vz59T is a AFV machine gun and this is fitted to the OT-62 and OT-810 APCs.

Below: *The Vz59 General Purpose Machine Gun.*

7.62mm Vzor 52(Vz52) and Vzor 52/57(Vz52/57) Light Machine Gun

Czechoslovakia

Calibre: 7.62mm
Length: 104.5cm
Length of Barrel: 58.3cm
Weight: 8.7kg(with loaded magazine)
8.3kg(with empty magazine)
8kg(without magzine)
Magazine Capacity: 25-round box or a 100-round belt
Range: 800m
Rate of Fire: 900rpm(cyclic) box magazine
1 140 rpm(cyclic) belt fed
150rpm(practical)

Note—data relates to the Vz52/57

Below: *The Vz52/57 Light Machine Gun.*

The Vz52 was introduced into service in 1952 and was a development of the earlier Vz26 weapon (similar to the British Bren). The Vz52 is a selective fire, gas-operated, air-cooled weapon. Its barrel can be quickly changed, if required the gun can be mounted on a tripod in place of its normal bipod. The Vz52 fires the Czech 7.62mm × 45 M52 cartridge with a m/v of 755m/s. It has no selector as such, the rate of fire being determined by the position of the gunner's finger on the trigger, the upper part of the trigger (marked 1) for single shots and the lower part of the trigger (marked D) for full automatic. Yet another feature of the Vz52 is that it is cocked by pulling the pistol grip to the rear. The foresight is of the blade type and the rearsight is of the tangent type with a U-notch, this is graduated from 200 to 1 200m in increments of 100m.

The Vz52 is no longer in front line service with the Czech Army.

In 1957 the Vz52/57 was introduced into service; this fires the 7.62mm × 39R cartridge with a m/v of 732m/s. Accessories for these weapons include a fabric sling, magazine carrier, belt boxes, combination tool and a cleaning rod. The Vz52/59 was replaced in front line units from 1959/60 with the 7.62mm Vz59 GPMG.

7.92mm ZB-26 & ZB-30 Light Machine Guns — Czechoslovakia

Calibre: 7.92mm
Length: 116.3cm
Length of Barrel: 61cm
Weight: 9.6kg(with loaded magazine)
9.1kg(with empty magazine)
8.9kg(without magazine)
Magazine Capacity: 20 rounds
Range: 800m
Rate of Fire: 500rpm(cyclic)
180rpm(practical)

Note—Data relates to the ZB-26

The ZB-26 was issued to the Czechoslovakian Army before the start of the World War 2 and was also used as the basis for the Bren LMG. The Czechs continued to use this weapon after the war until it was replaced by the Vz52 LMG. The weapon fires the 7.92mm × 57 cartridge with a m/v of 810m/s. The gun is gas operated and air-cooled and can fire both on full automatic or single-shot. Its front sight is of the blade type and its rearsight is of the adjustable aperture type. Both the ZB-26 and the ZB-30 were used by the Germans during World War 2 as they continued production of the gun. The ZB-26 was also built for export as the ZB-30 whose most obvious modification was that it could be fitted with a monopod in a socket in the stock. The ZB-30 was also built in China as the Type 26 Light Machine Gun; in addition Iran and Romania built the weapon. Yugoslavia also built the ZB-30. The ZB-26 is recognisable by its flash eliminator, ribbed barrel, gas cylinder under the barrel, bipod, carrying handle above the barrel and in front of the vertical magazine and the barrel locking handle on the LHS of the weapon.

Below: *The top weapon in this photograph is the ZB-26 LMG whilst the lower weapon is the British Bren LMG which was developed from it.*

7.92mm ZB-37 Machine Gun — Czechoslovakia

Calibre: 7.92mm
Length: 110.5cm
Length of Barrel: 74cm(with flash eliminator)
67.8cm(barrel only)
Weight: 39kg(gun and tripod)
19kg(gun only)
Magazine Capacity: Fed from 100- or 200-round metallic non-disintegrating link belt
Range: 1 000m(maximum effective)
Rate of Fire: 750rpm(high setting)
500rpm(low setting)
200rpm(practical)

The ZB-37 was introduced into service with the Czech Army in 1937 and was used by them after the war. It is no longer in service with any of the Warsaw Pact Forces but it did turn up in the fighting in Nigeria a few years ago. The Germans used the weapon during the World War 2 and called it the MG 37(t), the British adopted the weapon for use as a tank machine gun under the name Besa but this is no longer in service with the British Army. The ZB-37 fires the 7.92 × 57mm cartridge with a m/v of 793m/s. Its foresight is of the blade type and its rearsight is of the leaf type graduated from 300 to 2 000m. The weapon can be found with both a smooth or a ribbed barrel and there are two types of tripod.

82mm Recoilless Gun T-21(Tarasnice) — Czechoslovakia

Calibre: 82mm
Weight of Launcher(Travelling): 20kg(with wheel mount)
Weight of Launcher(Firing): 17.2kg(without wheel mount)
Length of Tube: 147.5cm
Range: 280m(moving target)
Rate of Fire: 4–6rpm
Crew: 2

The T-21 is an electrically-fired, smooth-bore breech-loaded recoilless weapon that can be fired from the ground using the two small detachable wheels for support or from the shoulder whilst standing or in the prone position. The weapon has also been mounted externally on the turrets of the OT-62 armoured personnel carrier and the OT-65 reconnaissance vehicle.

It is recognisable by its two small wheels, the towing handle that folds back along the tube at the front and the two pistol type grips.

The weapon fires a fin-stabilised HEAT projectile which has a Z-21 fuze. The projectile weighs 2.13kg, has a muzzle velocity of 250m/s and will penetrate 230mm of armour. The T-21 is provided with two sights on the LHS, one is optical and the other is mechanical. The optical sight is marked from 100 to 600m in 100m intervals whilst the mechanical sight is marked from 100 to 600m in 50m intervals.

Since the breechblock has no extractor, the loader must either shake out the expended case or extract it with the aid of an asbestos glove.

Below: *The 82mm T-21 Tarasnice Recoilless Gun.*

Anti-Tank Grenade Launcher P-27 (Pancerovka) — Czechoslovakia

Calibre: 45mm(tube)
Weight of Launcher: 6.4kg
Length of Tube: 103cm
Range: 100m(stationary targets)
75mm(moving targets)
Rate of Fire: 4–6rpm
Crew: 2

The P-27 is the Czech equivalent of the Russian RPG-2 weapon. The ammunition cannot be used in the Soviet weapon, however. It is a smooth-bore, muzzle-loaded, recoilless weapon and its recognition features are its bipod which unfolds, pistol type grip and folding sights.

The HEAT round is not rocket-assisted and is 720mm in length and weighs 3.75kg; the projectile weighs 3.3kg and has a muzzle velocity of 75m/s and will penetrate 250mm of armour.

The sights are marked for 50, 75, 100, 125 and 150m and the firing mechanism is by electricity generated by a magneto. The P-27 has been replaced in front line Czech units by the Soviet RPG-7V weapon.

Below: *The P-27 (Pancerovka) Anti-Tank Grenade Launcher.*

9mm Madsen Model 50 and 53 Sub-Machine Guns — Denmark

Model 50

Calibre: 9mm
Length Stock Extended: 79.37cm
Length Stock Folded: 52.83cm
Length of Barrel: 19.8cm
Weight Empty: 3.2kg
Magazine Capacity: 32 rounds
Muzzle Velocity: 390m/s
Maximum Effective Range: 100m
Rate of Fire: 550rpm(cyclic)

The Madsen Model 50 and 53 are basically similar and have a number of unusual design features. One is the method of stripping which is affected by removing the magazine and barrel nut when the two receiver halves then open sideways on two hinges at the rear. The magazine can be filled using a filler-guide carried in the pistol grip. Both types were developed from the earlier Model 1946 and both have been sold to various forces around the world including Chile.

A version of the Madsen is made in Brazil as the Metralhadora de MAO 0.45 in INA 953. This version, apart from the 0.45in calibre, differs in many respects from the original but is visually similar. It is used by the Brazilian Army and police.

Bottom left: *The 9mm Madsen Model 50 Sub-Machine Gun.*

9mm Lahti M35 Pistol

Finland

Calibre: 9mm
Length: 24.6cm
Length of Barrel: 10.7cm
Weight: 1.22kg
Magazine Capacity: 8 rounds
Muzzle Velocity: 350m/s
Maximum Effective Range: 40m

Despite the fact that it was first accepted for service in 1935, the Lahti is still in service in Finland, and is also still in use in Sweden where it is known as the P.40 or M.40. The mechanism of the Lahti is very reliable and well-sealed to keep out dirt and grit but it is a very difficult weapon to strip—two factors which may explain its longevity.

Above: *The 9mm Lahti M35 Pistol.*

9mm Model 1944 Sub-Machine Gun — Finland

Calibre: 9mm
Length—Stock Extended: 83.1cm
Length—Stock Folded: 62.2cm
Weight Loaded(36 round mag): 3.59kg
Weight Loaded(71 round drum): 4.27kg
Weight Empty: 2.9kg
Magazine Capacity: 36-round box
71-round drum
Muzzle Velocity: 399m/s
Maximum Effective Range: 200m
Rate of Fire: 650rpm(cyclic)

The Model 1944 was a Finnish copy of the Russian PPS-43 to take the 9mm Parabellum round and it was built in Finland in large quantities before the war ended. In appearance it differs little from the Russian original, but in Finnish Army service it is usually used with the 36-round box magazine—the 50-round Suomi and 71-round Russian magazines may also be used. The designer later took the drawings to Spain where the type was made at Oviedo as the Dux SMG. This weapon was licence-built by Mauser and later Anshutz for the West German Border Guard where it is still in use in small numbers.

9mm Model 1931 (m/31) Sub-Machine Gun — Finland

Calibre: 9mm
Length: 87cm
Length of Barrel: 31.8cm
Weight: 7.09kg with 71-round magazine
4.68kg without magazine
Magazine Capacity: 50-round box or
71-round drum
Muzzle Velocity: 399m/s
Effective Range: 200m
Rate of Fire: 900rpm(cyclic)
120rpm(automatic)
40rpm(single shots)

The Model 1931 Sub-Machine Gun was made in Finland by Oy Tikkakoski and was subsequently adopted by a number of countries including Norway, Sweden and Switzerland (known as the MP 43/44).

Its system of operation is of the blowback type and it fires a standard 9mm parabellum cartridge. The firer can select either full automatic fire or single shots.

Below: *A Finnish soldier using his m/31 Sub-Machine Gun with a 71-round drum type magazine.*

7.62mm M60 and M62 Assault Rifles — Finland

Calibre: 7.62mm
Length: 91.4cm
Length of Barrel: 42cm
Weight Loaded: 4.7kg
Weight Empty: 3.5kg
Magazine Capacity: 30 rounds
Muzzle Velocity: 719m/s
Maximum Effective Range: 350-400m
Rate of Fire: 650rpm(cyclic)
120rpm(auto)
40rpm(single shots)

During the late 1950's the Finnish Valmet concern acquired a manufacturing licence to make the Russian AK-47 assault rifle. Before the weapon could be accepted by the Finnish Army some changes were called for and the result was the M60. This differs from the AK-47 in having no trigger-guard (to accommodate winter mittens), no wooden furniture (all the stocks and grips are plastic) and revised sights. Another change is the tubular butt. The M62 differs in small detail, the most noticeable of which is the re-introduction of the trigger-guard.

Below: *The Finnish 7.62mm M62 Assault Rifle.*

7.62mm KK62 Light Machine Gun — Finland

Calibre: 7.62mm
Length: 108.5cm
Length of Barrel: 47cm
Weight Unloaded: 8.3kg
Weight Loaded: 10.6kg
Type of Feed: 100-round belt
Muzzle Velocity: 730m/s
Maximum Effective Range: 350-450m
Rate of Fire: 1 000-1 100rpm(cyclic)
300rpm(practical)

Despite the lack of external similarities, the KK62 is based on the mechanism of the Czech ZB26 light machine gun. It entered service with the Finnish Army in 1966 and is used by no other country. For an LMG the KK62 has a high rate of fire and is also unusual in feeding the 7.62mm × 39 Russian cartridge belts from the RHS. Only full automatic fire is possible—there is no facility for single shots. No trigger-guard is fitted in line with Finnish practice to allow for the use of thick gloves by the firer.

Above: *The soldier on the left is firing the 7.62mm KK62 Light Machine Gun.*

Type m/55 Anti-Tank Grenade Launcher — Finland

Calibre: 55mm
Length: 94cm(without grenade)
124cm(with grenade)
Weight: 6.5kg(launcher only)
2.5kg(grenade)
Effective Range: 300m
Rate of Fire: 3–5rpm

The m/55 is the standard light anti-tank weapon of the Finnish Army and is similar in some respects to the Soviet RPG-7 launcher. The sight is on the LHS with the handle and firing trigger in the centre; at the rear is the venturi. The HEAT grenade is reported to be able to penetrate 300mm of armour at 300m.

Below: *The Finnish Type m/55 Anti-Tank Grenade Launcher.*

9mm PAP Mle F1 France

Calibre: 9mm
Length: 234mm
Length of Barrel: 150mm
Weight Empty: 1.215kg
Magazine Capacity: 15 rounds
Muzzle Velocity: 350m/s
Maximum Effective Range: 50m

The 9mm PAP Mle F1 is the service version of the 9mm MAB P15s. It is a remarkable service pistol in that it has a 15-round magazine which together with the long barrel employed make it a very good target pistol. As well as being in service with the French Army it is also used by the French Air Force.

9mm MAS Model 1950 Pistol France

Above: *The 9mm MAS Model 1950 Pistol.*

Calibre: 9mm
Length: 195mm
Length of Barrel: 111mm
Weight Empty: 0.81kg
Weight Loaded: 1.04kg
Magazine Capacity: 9 rounds
Muzzle Velocity: 354m/s
Maximum Effective Range: 50m

As well as being in service with the French Army, the Model 1950 is also in use with the French Gendarmerie and Police.

9mm MAT 49 Sub-Machine Gun — France

Calibre: 9mm
Length—Butt Extended: 71cm
Length—Butt Retracted: 55.8cm
Weight Loaded: 4.76kg
Magazine Capacity: 32 rounds
Muzzle Velocity: 354m/s
Maximum Effective Range: 200m
Rate of Fire: 600rpm(cyclic)

The MAT 49 is made from heavy gauge steel pressings and features an unusual magazine which can be folded forward to reduce bulk when carried. A grip safety is employed so there is no safety catch. The MAT 49 is now the standard SMG of the French forces, and is still in use by some of the former French Colonies in Africa. The Vietnamese have converted some MAT 49s to fire the Soviet 7.62 × 25 cartridge.

Below: *The 9mm MAT 49 Sub-Machine Gun.*

5.56mm MAS Automatic Rifle — France

Calibre: 5.56mm
Length: 75.7cm
Length of Barrel: 48.8cm
Weight Less Magazine and Extras: 3.38kg
Magazine Capacity: 25 rounds
Muzzle Velocity: 960m/s
Maximum Effective Range: 300m
Rate of Fire: 900–1 000rpm(cyclic)

The MAS rifle is a new design using a 'bullpup' configuration with optional ejection to left or right. The large handle over the barrel also acts as a protective cover for the sights. This handle and the butt are both plastic. The trigger mechanism can be set to either single shot or automatic but an extra mode can be selected that fires a three-round burst every time the trigger is pressed. Bipod legs can be fitted and grenades can also be fired. At the time of writing it had not been announced whether the MAS rifle was to become the standard French service arm, but it would appear to be very likely.

Top right: *The 5.56mm MAS Automatic Rifle.*

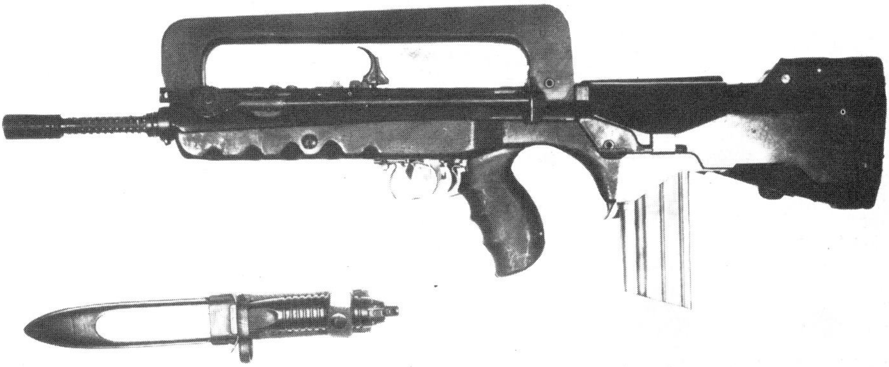

FR-F1 Sniper's Rifle

France

Calibre: 7.5mm and 7.62mm
Length(Variable): 113.8cm
Weight Empty: 5.2kg
Magazine Capacity: 10 rounds
Muzzle Velocity: 852m/s
Maximum Effective Range: 800m

The FR-F1, or Fusil a Repetition Modele F1, is a version of the pre-war Model 1936 rifle modified to take telescopic sights for use by snipers. It has a manual bolt action and butt spacers can be fitted to the butt to suit individual requirements. To suit the snjper role, two extras are a bipod and a flash hider. Some of these rifles were produced in 7.62mm calibre.

Below: *The French 7.5mm FR-F1 Sniper's Rifle with bipod and telescopic sight.*

7.5mm Model 49/56 Rifle

France

Calibre: 7.5mm
Length: 101cm
Length of Barrel: 52.1cm
Weight Loaded: 4.34kg
Magazine Capacity: 10 rounds
Muzzle Velocity: 817m/s
Maximum Effective Range: 600m

The MAS 49/56 self-loading rifle was developed from the earlier Model 49 from which it differs in having a shortened fore-stock and a combined flash hider and grenade launcher. It is at present the standard French service rifle and it is also used in many former French Dependencies. The earlier Model 49 also remains in widespread use. A telescopic sight can be fitted. Some Model 49/56 rifles were produced in NATO 7.62mm calibre.

Above: *The 7·5mm Model 49/56 Rifle with night viewing system.*

7.5mm AA 52 Machine Gun

France

Calibre: 7.5mm and 7.62mm
Length—Light Barrel: 114.5cm
Length of Light Barrel: 50cm
Length of Heavy Barrel: 60cm
Weight with Light Barrel/Bipod: 10.7kg
Type of Feed: Continuous link belts
Muzzle Velocity: 800m/s
Maximum Range: 3 000m
Rate of Fire: 800rpm(cyclic)

The 'Arme Automatique Transformable Mle 1952' is the standard French machine gun and is unusual in many respects. It uses a form of retarded blowback action and is one of the very few machine guns to employ this type of action with a full-power cartridge. As a result the chamber walls are fluted for ease of extraction but examination of fired cartridges will often show distortion or even breakage. The general standard of manufacture shows that the weapon has been designed for low cost and many stampings are used. In the LMG role a light barrel and bipod are used—this is the Fusil-Mitrailleur N-F1. As a sustained fire weapon the gun is fitted with a heavy barrel and mounted on a tripod. In both roles the gun can fire automatic only. As an LMG the gun can be laid on fixed lines by the use of a telescopic monopod leg under the butt. The AA 52 has been produced in both 7.5 and 7.62mm calibres.

Above: *The 7.5mm AA 52 Machine Gun.*

ARPAC Anti-Tank Weapon — France

Calibre: 72mm
Weight: 1.25kg
Length: 55cm(firing)
40cm(transport)
Range: 50–80m
Crew: 1

The ARPAC (Arme Individuelle de Proximité Anti-Char) has been under the direction of GIAT at its MAS (Manufacture Nationale d'Armes de Saint-Etienne) establishment. Its two main features are that it hardly makes any noise when fired and it has no rear blast effect.

The launcher is constructed of plastic materials and glass resin compounds. The ammunition is of the shaped charge type and as soon as it leaves the launcher the motor ignites. The initial m/v is only 7m/s and this increases to 76m/s in 10m; time of flight to 50m is .86 of a second and to 80m, 1.32 seconds. The complete round of ammunition is 25cm in length, weighs .7kg, and will penetrate 250mm of armour at 0° angle of incidence.

Above: *The ARPAC Anti-Tank Weapon.*

ACL/APX-80 Anti-Tank Weapon — France

Calibre: 80mm
Weight: 16.44kg(loaded)
13kg(unloaded)
Length: 140cm
Range: 550m
Crew: 1

The ACL/APX-80 anti-tank weapon has been developed under the direction of the Groupement Industriel des Armements Terrestres (GIAT); in 1973 it was said to be entering production.

After the round is fired a sustainer charge ignites and this enables it to achieve a range of 550m in 1.2 seconds. The following types of ammunition have been developed—anti-personnel, anti-tank, illuminating and smoke. The anti-tank round weighs 3.75kg, is 530mm in length, and according to GIAT, will penetrate a double NATO heavy tank target.

Above: *The ACL /APX-80 Anti-Tank Weapon.*

SARPAC 68mm Anti-Tank Rocket Launcher France

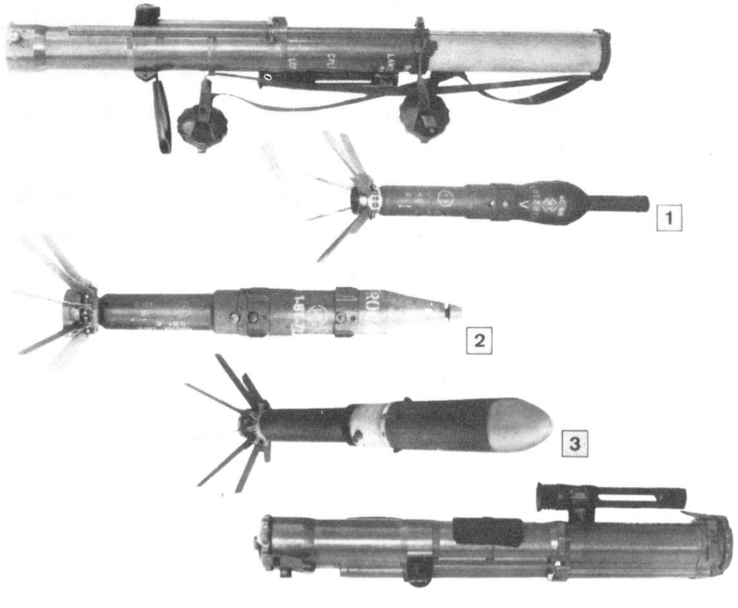

Calibre: 68mm
Total Weight(Carrying, with rocket): 2.67kg
Total Weight(Ready for action, with rocket) 2.35kg
Length(Carrying): 73.4cm
Length(Ready for action): 99.7cm
Range: 150–200m
Crew: 1 or 2

The SARPAC is a light infantry support weapon which is manufactured by Hotchkiss-Brandt. When required for action the covers at either end of the barrel are removed, the barrel is extended and the sights raised. When firing anti-personel and illuminating rockets an additional telescope is used, as these are fired at an angle of up to 40°.

The following fin-stabilised rockets are available for the SARPAC launcher:-Rochar anti-tank rocket weighing 1.07kg. This 472mm in length and has a range of 200m; muzzle velocity is 150m/s and its shaped charged warhead will penetrate 300mm of armour. Like the anti-personnel rocket, the anti-tank rocket is not armed until it is 10/12m out of the launcher.

Rocap anti-personnel rocket weighing 1.8kg, has a maximum range of 630m and has good fragmentation.

Roclair illuminating rocket weighing 1.3kg, will illuminate a 300m diameter zone for 30 seconds with an average power of 180 000 Candelas.

Bottom left: *The SARPAC 68mm Anti-Tank Launcher: top shows the launcher ready for action, No. 1 is the Rochar anti-tank rocket, No. 2 is the Rocap anti-personnel rocket and No. 3 is the Roclair illuminating rocket, the bottom photograph shows the SARPAC ready for carrying.*

Strim 89mm Anti-Tank Rocket Launcher — France

Calibre: 88.9mm
Total Weight(Carrying): 4.5kg(including telescope)
Total Weight(Ready for action): 7.3kg
Length(Carrying): 116.8cm
Length(Ready for action): 160cm
Range: 200m–600m(practical)
2 300m maximum at 45° angle
Crew: 2

This weapon has been developed by Luchaire SA and is manufactured in co-operation with the Manufacture Nationale d'Armes de Saint-Etienne, and is marketed by Hotchkiss-Brandt.

The rocket launcher itself is of glass fibre construction and is reusable.

When required for action a rocket in its container is attached to the rear of the launcher, as this is done the firing circuit is connected. The rocket is kept in a sealed container which is 626mm in length and weighs a total of 3.2kg. The rocket itself weighs 2.2kg and has a shaped charge warhead 80mm in diameter. The rocket has a muzzle velocity of 300m/s and will, according to the manufacturers, penetrate 400m of armour or 1 300mm of concrete.

As the rocket leaves the launcher nine stabilisers unfold and these stablise the rocket in flight. Flight time to 330m = 1.25 seconds and flight time to 360m = 1.36 seconds.

The STRIM is fitted with the APX M 290 sighting system which is graduated from 0 to 1 000m, a passive telescope for night action is also available. Other rockets available apart from the basic anti-tank model, are a practice rocket, an illuminating rocket, an incendiary rocket and the AVL light anti-tank rocket.

Above: *The STRIM 89mm Anti-Tank Rocket Launcher together with rocket, this has its stabilisers extended.*

Hotchkiss-Brandt 60mm Light Mortar (MO-60-63)

France

Calibre: 60mm
Total Weight: 14.8kg
Barrel Weight: 3.8kg
Bipod Weight: 5kg
Baseplate Weight: 6kg
Length of Barrel: 72.4cm(including breech)
Elevation: + 40° to + 85°
Traverse: 300mils
Range: 100m(minimum)
2 050m(maximum)
Crew: 3

The MO-60-63 is manufactured by the Armament Department of Hotchkiss-Brandt. It has been designed so that it can be broken down into three-man pack loads for easy transportation: barrel, bipod and baseplate. This mortar can fire the old 60mm Brandt bombs and the 60mm American bombs. Hotchkiss-Brandt manufacture the following bombs for it:
HE bomb Mk. 61, this has a V 9 fuse and weighs 1.78kg.
HE Coloured Bomb—green, yellow or red.
Smoke Bomb Mk. 61.
Practice Bomb—Two types.
Illuminating Bomb Mk. 61, weight 1.55kg, 180 000 candelas.
The bombs have a primary and secondary charge system which gives six charges, ie charge 0 = 100m range and charge 5 = 2 050m range normal rate of fire is 20rpm although 30rpm can be fired for short periods. These bombs are also used with the Hotchkiss-Brandt 60mm Commando Mortar, but with this weapon No. 2 charge is the maximum that can be used.

Below: *The Hotchkiss-Brandt 60mm Light Mortar in the assembled position.*
Top right: *A selection of the Hotchkiss-Brandt 60mm mortar bombs.*

Hotchkiss-Brandt 60mm Commando Mortar France

Calibre: 60mm
Total Weight: 7.7kg(automatic model)
Overall Length: 68cm(automatic model)
Length of Barrel: 65cm(automatic model)
Total Weight: 10kg(controlled firing model)
Overall Length: 86.1cm(controlled firing model)
Length of Barrel: 65cm(controlled firing model)
Range: 100m(minimum)
1 050m(maximum)
Crew: 2

This light hand-held weapon is manufactured by the Armament Department of Hotchkiss-Brandt. It consists of the following parts — barrel, breech, baseplate, protective sleeve, muzzle cover and carrying strap. The weapon is normally carried fully assembled with the aid of the strap. It fires the same bombs as the Hotchkiss-Brandt 60mm Light Mortar (MO-60-63) (cf.) For use with the Commando mortar three charges are used 0, 1 and 2, ie charge 0 = 100m range and charge 2 = 1 050m range. Charge 3 can be used in 'exceptional circumstances.'

The weapon is normally loaded, aimed and fired from the lying or kneeling position. Two models are available, the automatic model and the controlled firing model. The difference between the two models is that the standard model(automatic)

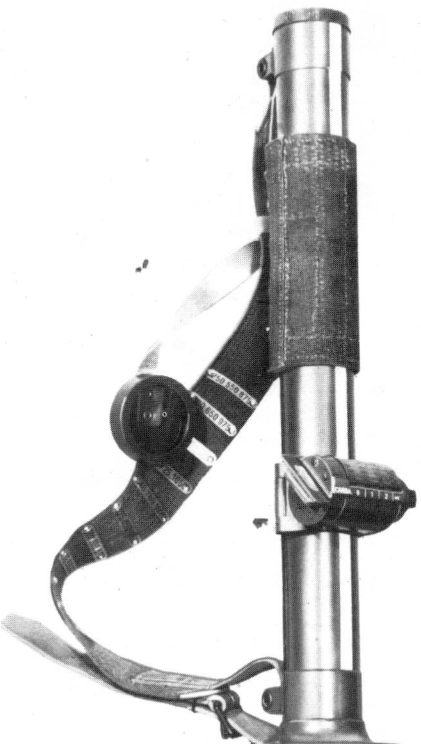

Right: *The Hotchkiss-Brandt 60mm Commando Mortar (automatic model).*

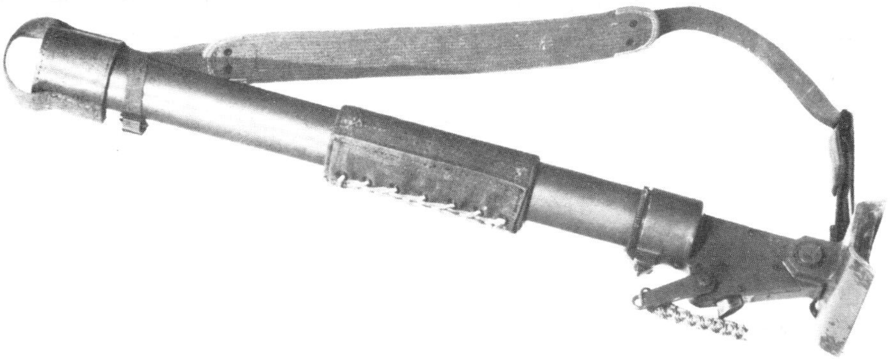

is fired as a normal mortar, ie the bomb is dropped down the barrel where it hits a firing pin and is then fired. In the controlled model the bomb is dropped down the barrel and is fired when required by pressing the trigger.

The standard model has a simple clinometer and range table which the controlled model does not have.

The controlled model is laid by aligning a white line painted along the top of the barrel, with the target or aiming mark and the barrel raised or lowered to the correct elevation. Maximum range for any charge is achieved with the barrel at an angle of 45°.

Above: *The Hotchkiss-Brandt 60mm Commando Mortar (controlled firing model).*

Walther 9mm P1

Germany(FGR)

Calibre: 9mm
Length: 218mm
Length of Barrel: 124mm
Weight Loaded: 960gr
Magazine Capacity: 8 rounds
Muzzle Velocity: 360m/s
Maximum Effective Range: 50m

The P1 is the modern version of the wartime Walther P38 which was the standard Wehrmacht pistol—numbers of the these weapons manufactured before 1945 remain in use with various nations around the world (eg Yugoslavia). The P1 differs from the P38 in having a lighter receiver and a different firing pin. It is the standard service pistol of West Germany, Norway, Portugal and Chile and is a popular weapon with many police forces.

Below: *The Walther 9mm P1 pistol.*

Walther 7.65mm PP and PPK

Germany(FGR)

Model PP
Calibre: 7.65 and 9mm
Length: 173mm
Length of Barrel: 99mm
Weight: 682g
Magazine Capacity: 8 rounds—PPK 7 rounds
Muzzle Velocity(7.65mm): 290m/s
Maximum Effective Range: 40m

The PP first appeared in 1929 and ever since has been a popular pistol for both police and military duties. It remains in service with Hungary, Guyana and the United Kingdom both as a service arm and as a military police pistol. It is made in Turkey where it is known as the MKE Kirikkale and until recently was licence-made by Manuhrin in France. The PPK is a smaller 'pocket' pistol using the same basic mechanism which is still used by many police and service arms. The Hungarians call it the 7.65mm M48 pistol.

Below: *The 7.65mm PPK pistol which is made in Germany by Carl Walther of Ulm.*

9mm Pistol M1908

Germany

Calibre: 9mm
Length: 22cm
Length of Barrel: 10cm
Weight Loaded: .988kg
Weight Empty: .89kg
Magazine Capacity: 8 rounds
Muzzle Velocity: 322m/s
Effective Range: 50m

This is the world-famous Luger pistol. The first model entered production in 1898 in 7.65mm calibre. Later models came in 1900, 1902, 1904 and 1908, but the Luger was replaced in the German Army from 1938 by the Walther P 38. The weapon is still in service in many countries and is now being manufactured for commercial sales by Mauser-Werke GMBH of Oberndorf, West Germany. Its method of operation is of the short recoil type and it fires the 9mm parabellum round.

It is recognisable by its distinctive and unique toggle-locking system with two milled knobs on the top of the receiver, a square plate above the trigger on the LHS, and a semi-circular recess cut in the bottom of the grip to receive the circular magazine button.

The foresight is of the blade type and the rear-sight is of the open V-notch type.

Above: *The 9mm Luger Model M1908 pistol.*

Heckler and Koch 9mm MP5 Sub-Machine Gun

Germany(FGR)

MP5A2
Calibre: 9mm
Length: 68cm
Length of Barrel: 22.5cm
Weight Loaded: 2.94kg
Magazine Capacity: 10, 15 or 30 rounds
Muzzle Velocity: 400m/s
Maximum Effective Range: 200-300m
Rate of Fire: 650rpm(cyclic)
100rpm(automatic)
50rpm(single shot)

The MP5 was at one time known as the HK54 and it is a shortened version of the Heckler and Koch G3 rifle with which it shares many interchangeable components. The basic MP5 is fitted with a fixed plastic stock as the MP5A2 while the MP5A3 has a sliding metal stock. Both versions can be fitted with a .22 cub-calibre training device and the MP5SD is a silenced version. In all its forms the MP5 is regarded as one of the most accurate sub-machine guns available and accuracy is improved on some recent production versions by the fitting of a mechanism that restricts bursts to three rounds on automatic. All the MP5 weapons make extensive use of nylon and plastic furniture and steel stampings. They are used by German Police and para-military units, and some have been sold to small armies abroad.

Below: *The Heckler & Koch 9mm MP5A2 Sub-Machine Gun.*
Top right: *The Heckler & Koch 9mm MP5A3 Sub-Machine Gun.*

Walther MP-L and MP-K Sub-Machine Guns

Germany(FGR)

MP-K
Calibre: 9mm
Length—Stock Extended: 65.3cm
Length—Stock Folded: 36.8cm
Length of Barrel: 17.1cm
Weight Loaded: 3.425kg
Magazine Capacity: 32 rounds
Muzzle Velocity: 356m/s
Maximum Effective Range: 200m
Rate of Fire: 550rpm

The Walther MP-L and MP-K differ only in the length of barrel fitted with the -L version having the longer barrel. Both were first produced in 1963 and were procured for police and naval units in Germany.

Below: *The Walther MP-L Sub-Machine Gun.*

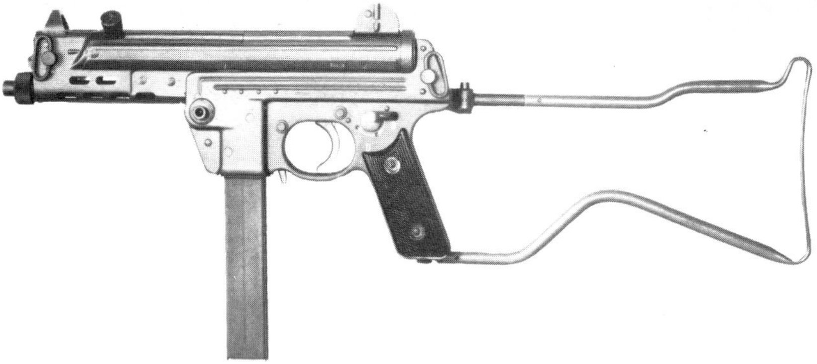

Above: *The Walther MP-K Sub-Machine Gun.*

9mm MP40 Sub-Machine Gun — Germany(FGR)

Calibre: 9mm
Length—Stock Extended: 83.3cm
Length—Stock Folded: 63cm
Length of Barrel: 25.1cm
Weight Loaded: 4.7kg
Magazine Capacity: 32 rounds
Muzzle Velocity: 381m/s
Maximum Effective Range: 200m
Rate of Fire: 500rpm(cyclic)

The MP40 was developed from the MP38 and MP38/40 and during the war it was produced in very large numbers. After 1945 it remained in service with many nations but today it is used by very few armed forces. Norway is one exception where the MP40 is called the Maskin 9mm M40. The MP40 is still a popular weapon with many irregular and guerrilla organisations and has been encountered in Vietnam and in various African states.

Below: *The 9mm MP 40 Sub-Machine Gun.*

4.6mm HK36 Assault Rifle — Germany(FGR)

Calibre: 4.6mm
Length: 88.9cm(butt extended)
76.9cm(butt retracted)
Length of Barrel: 38.1cm
Weight: 3.67kg(with 90 rounds)
2.849kg(empty)
Magazine Capacity: 30 or 90 rounds
Range: 300m
Rate of Fire: 1100/1200rpm(cyclic)
90/180rpm(practical)

The HK36 assault rifle has been designed by Heckler and Koch. Although it has been tested by the German Army it is not yet in production.

The weapon fires a 4.6mm × 36 round. Two types of cartridge have been developed, one with a conventional lead core(m/v 850m/s)and the other with a tungston-carbide core(m/v 777m/s). It is recoil-operated and its bolt system is of the delayed roller locked type. The selector is on the left side and the settings are for safe, single-shot and full automatic, the latter giving controlled bursts of 2–5 rounds. The HK36 has a reflex sight with daylight screen and a betalight for twilight operations.

The main advantage of the weapon is its light weight. For example the HK36 assault rifle with 500 rounds is equivalent to a standard German Army 7.62mm G3 rifle with 100 rounds of ammunition. The 4.6mm ammunition has greater penetration performance and an asymmetrical point.

Below: *The 4.6mm HK 36 Assault Rifle.*

Heckler and Koch HK33 Rifle

Germany(FGR)

Calibre: 5.56mm
Length(Butt Stock): 92cm
Length(Retracted Stock): 75cm
Length(Carbine, Retracted Stock): 67cm
Length of Barrel: 39cm
Length of Barrel(Carbine): 32.2cm
Weight(HK33A2): 3.35kg
Magazine Capacity: 20 or 40 rounds
Muzzle Velocity: 960m/s
Maximum Effective Range: 400m
Rate of Fire: 600-650rpm(cyclic)
100rpm(automatic)
40rpm(single shot)

The HK33 is a member of the Heckler and Koch Group 2 family of weapons—Group 1 firing the NATO 7.62mm round and Group 3 firing the Russian 7.62mm round. Group 2 weapons all fire the American 5.56mm × 45 round and the HK33 can be fitted with a 20 or 40-round magazine. The HK33A2 has a rigid butt stock and the HK33A3 uses a telescopic butt. The HK33A2 fitted with a telescopic sight is known as the HK33ZF. There is a carbine version with a telescopic stock known as the HK33KA or HK33KA1. The full range of Heckler and Koch accessories can be fitted to all versions except that the carbine version cannot be

Above: *The Heckler and Koch HK33A2 Rifle.*

used to fire the 40mm grenade. Although not selected for Bundeswehr use the HK33 is in limited production by GIAT in France and also made in Saudi Arabia. Malaysia has bought 5 000. Heckler & Koch have also developed an assault rifle known as the HK36 which fires a new 4.6mm round but it has not been adopted for service.

The Heckler and Kock Group 2 family of weapons is completed by the HK13 and HK23/HK23A1 machine guns and HK53 sub-machine gun, but none of these weapons has yet been adopted either.

Above: *The Heckler and Koch HK33A3 Rifle.*

Heckler and Koch G3 Rifle

Germany(FGR)

Calibre: 7.62mm
Length(Fixed Butt): 102cm
Length of Barrel: 45cm
Weight Loaded: 5kg
Magazine Capacity: 20 rounds
Muzzle Velocity: 780–800m/s
Maximum Effective Range: 400m
Rate of Fire: 500–600rpm(cyclic)
100rpm(automatic)
40rpm(single shot)

After 1945 a group of German designers produced the CETME automatic rifle in Spain, and the design was eventually produced by Heckler & Koch for the Bundeswehr as the Gewehr 3 or G3A3. The type has since been exported widely and produced under licence by a large number of countries (see below). There are some variations to the basic design as one version has a retracting butt (G3A4), and, when fitted with a telescopic sight, it is known as the G3A3ZF. (Singlepoint sights can also be fitted). There is a special sniper's version, the G3 SG/1, which differs in small details from the basic G3A3. Extensive use is made of plastic furniture and metal stamping in the design, and the G3 can be fitted with a bayonet, bipod, a sub-calibre training device, a 40mm muzzle-mounted grenade launcher and a special plastic blank round for training. Spain continues to produce the original version as the CETME Model 58.

Below: *The Heckler and Koch G3A3 Rifle.*

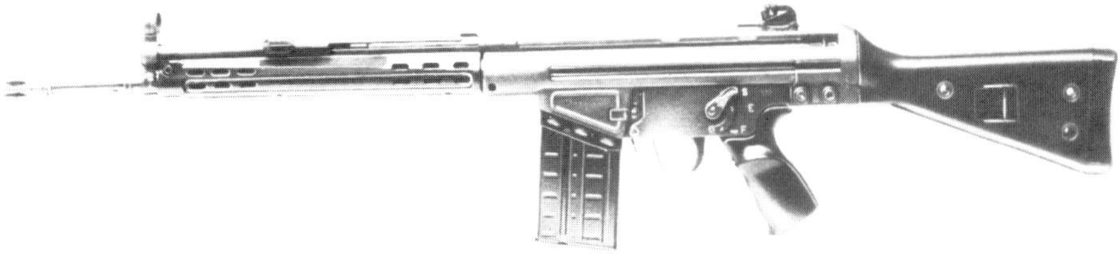

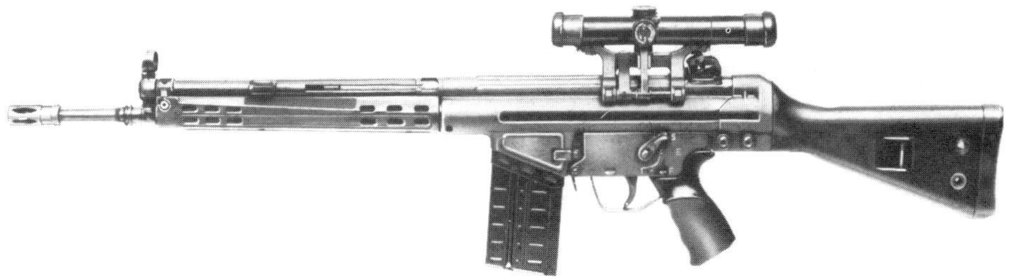

Producer Countries
Brazil, France, Iran, Malaysia, Norway, Pakistan, Portugal, Saudi Arabia, Sweden, Thailand, United Kingdom, West Germany.

User Countries
Abu Dhabi, Bolivia, Burma, Chad, Chile, Columbia, Denmark, Dominican Republic, Dubai, El Salvador, Ghana, Indonesia, Jordon, Kenya, Nigeria, Peru, Philippines, Qatar, Sharjah, Sudan, Tanzania, Turkey, Uganda, Zambia.

Above: *The Heckler and Koch G3A3ZF Rifle with telescopic sights.*
Below: *The Heckler and Koch G3A4 Rifle with retracting butt.*

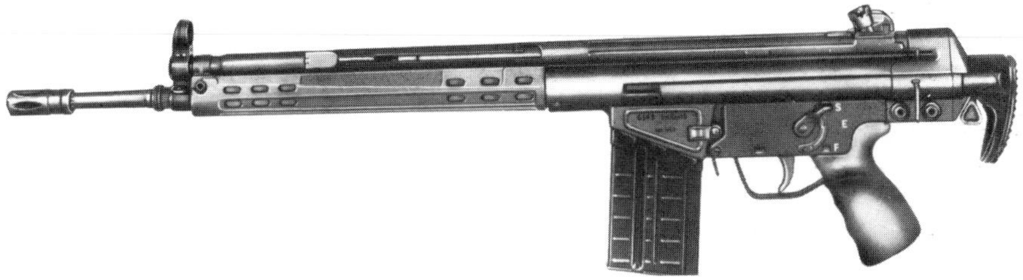

7.92mm MP-44 Assault Rifle — Germany

Calibre: 7.92mm
Overall Length: 93.3cm
Length of Barrel: 41.3cm
Weight Loaded: 5.2kg
Weight Empty: 4.5kg
Magazine Capacity: 30 rounds
Muzzle Velocity: 686m/s
Effective Range: 400m(semi-automatic)
200m(automatic)
Rate of Fire: 800rpm(cyclic)
100–120rpm(full automatic)
40–50rpm(semi-automatic)

This weapon can be said to be the forerunner of the modern assault rifle. Design of an assault rifle

Below: *The 7.92mm MP-44 Assault Rifle*

(automatic) started in Germany in 1938 and two companies built prototypes: Haenel, the MKb42 (H)) and Carl Walther, the MKb42(W). The MKb42 (H) was modified and became the MP-43 and later the MP-44(Sturmgewehr) and saw service in the last 18 months of WW2.

It is gas-operated and is capable of full and semi-automatic fire. Its front sight is of the hooded blade type and its rear sight is of the adjustable V-notch type. It fires the 7.92mm × 33 cartridge.

The weapon is still used by a number of countries including the East German Workers' Militia.

Mauser Model 98 Rifle — Germany

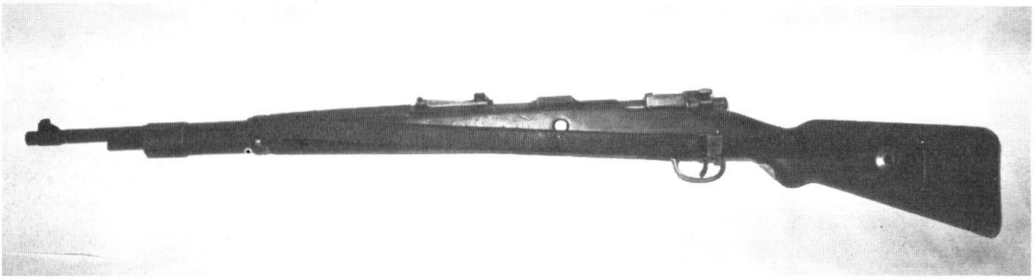

Kar 98k

Calibre: 7.92mm
Length: 111cm
Length of Barrel: 59.7cm
Weight Unloaded: 3.9kg
Magazine Capacity: 5 rounds
Muzzle Velocity: 754m/s
Maximum Effective Range: 600m(plus)

The Mauser Rifle has been in production since the 1880's in one form or another and it has the distinction of being produced in larger numbers than any other military rifle. Before and during WW2 the standard Wehrmacht rifle was the Karabiner 1898k or Kar 98k and this version was produced with minor variations by Czechoslovakia (vz.24), Belgium, Spain and other nations. After 1945 the Kar98k remained in use with many nations such as Czechoslovakia (until 1952), Portugal (as the /937), Norway, Spain, Indonesia and Albania. It is still reportedly in service in Albania, Norway, Spain and Yugoslavia (as the Puska 7.9mm, M-48), and many central American states. A copy manufactured after the war in Taiwan is known as the 7.92mm Rifle Model Chiang Kai-shek and Israel is known to have re-calibred some Kar 98ks to the 7.62mm NATO calibre. As a result of a large number of versions currently available on the second-hand market, this weapon is often encountered in the hands of irregular and guerrilla forces. There are many other types of Mauser rifle still in service, for example Mexico adopted the 7mm rifle in 1895 and other models were built in 1902, 1912 and 1936. The latter was similar in appearance to the American Springfield. The last model was the M1954 which was chambered for the American .30 cartridge.

Above: *The Mauser 7.92mm Model 98 Rifle.*

Heckler and Koch HK 21 Machine Gun — Germany(FGR)

Calibre: 7.62mm
Length with Butt: 102.1cm
Length Minus Butt: 82cm
Length of Barrel: 45cm
Weight with Bipod: 7.92kg
Type of Feed: 100-round belt or 20-round magazine
Muzzle Velocity: 800m/s
Maximum Effective Range: 1 200m
Rate of Fire: 850rpm(cyclic)
200rpm(practical)

The HK21 uses a number of G3 rifle components and has the same basic mechanism. It has been designed to carry out a number of roles and can have either a magazine feed or a belt feed from the left. It can be fired from a bipod or a tripod and the butt can be removed for mounting on or in vehicles. The standard weapon fires the 7.62mm × 51 NATO cartridge but by changing the barrel, bolt and bolt feed, the HK21 can fire the Russian 7.62mm × 39 cartridge. A similar change can be made for the 5.56mm × 45 round. A later version, the HK21A1, has a modified feed belt, and at the time of writing it seems likely that this version will be bought by Sweden. The HK21 is in service with the Portuguese Army only and has not been accepted for Bundeswehr use. An LMG version, the HK11, has yet to be sold anywhere.

Top right: *The Heckler and Koch HK 21 Machine Gun.*

7.62mm MG1 to MG3

Germany(FGR)

Calibre: 7.62mm
Length: 122.5cm
Length of Barrel: 53.1cm
Weight with Bipod: 11.5kg
Type of Feed: Belt
Muzzle Velocity: 820m/s
Maximum Effective Range(Bipod): 800m
Rate of Fire: 700–1 300rpm(cyclic)
250rpm(automatic)

When the 7.92mm MG42 entered service with the Wehrmacht in late 1942 it revolutionised machine gun design not only by its very efficient mechanism but by its construction which involved a maximum number of steel pressings and a minimum of costly machining processes. It also offered a fast barrel change. After the war the design was resurrected by Rheinmetall in the 7.62mm × 51 NATO calibre and in this form was offered commercially as the MG42/59. It was taken into Bundeswehr service as the MG1 and there were sub-variants such as the MG1A1, MG1A2, MG1A3, MG1A4 and MG1A5. These sub-variants had changes to the feed mechanism, muzzle booster and mountings. The MG2 was a conversion of war-production MG42s to the 7.62mm calibre. The MG3 is the latest version and has a number of changes, especially to the feed which can now cope with a wide range of ammunition belt eg the cartridge belt DM-1, disintegrating belts DN-13/3 and the

Below: *A MG42/59 of the Austrian Army.*

American M-13. The MG3 can be used on a bipod or tripod and can be fitted as a co-axial vehicle weapon as the MG3A1. A wide range of accessories can be used and special AA mounts are available. The MG3 is also produced in Italy, Spain, Pakistan and Portugal. It is used by the armed forces of West Germany, Austria(MG42 /59), Denmark(designated MG62), Chile (MG42 /59), Turkey, Norway (MG3), Iran(MG1A1) and the Sudan. The original MG42 is still encountered in the hands of irregular and guerrilla forces while the SARAC M53 is a Yugoslav version of the MG42 which is still produced in that country in the original 7.92mm and this version is virtually identical to the original.

Below: *The MG3 Machine Gun showing bipod and ammunition feed.*

Bottom: *MG3 Machine Gun team of the German Army.*

7.92mm MG34 Germany

Calibre: 7.92mm
Length: 122.4cm
Length of Barrel: 62.9cm
Weight of Tripod: 35kg
Weight of Bipod: 11.5kg
Type of Feed: 75-round drum or 50-round belt
Muzzle Velocity: 755m/s
Maximum Effective Range on Bipod: 600m
Maximum Effective Range on Tripod: 1 800–2 000m
Rate of Fire: 800–900rpm(cyclic)
300rpm(practical on tripod)
120rpm(practical on bipod)

The MG34 was one of the two standard machine guns of the Wehrmacht during WW2. It is no longer in front-line use anywhere but some are still used by the East German Militia and it forms the primary armament of the East German SK-1 Armoured Car which is used by para-military units. Some were reported to have been seen in action in Vietnam and Angola and a few were observed in the street fighting in Beirut in early 1976. The 7.92mm MG13 machine gun was seen in action during the Angolan war of early 1976.

Above: *The 7.92mm MG 34 Machine Gun on tripod.*

Armbrust 300 Anti-Tank Weapon Germany(FGR)

Calibre: 80mm
Weight: 6.3kg
Length: 85cm
Range: 300m
Crew: 1

The Armbrust 300 has been developed to prototype stage by Messerschmitt-Bolköw-Blohm of Ottobrunn and has been tested both in Germany and the United States. Boeing have a licence to manufacture the weapon if it is adopted by the United States Army.

The Armbrust has the following features—no firing report, no muzzle flash, no rear blast or flash or smoke. Its HEAT round will penetrate 300mm of armour plate and has a m/v of 220m/s, time to 300m is 1.5 seconds. The round is not armed until it is 7–12m from the weapon. Once fired

Armbrust is discarded. An illuminating round with a range of 1 000m is available as is a fragmentation round with a range of 500m.

The Armbrust consists of the sight, pistol trigger mechanism with cocking lever and safety, shoulder rest for firing in the standing or kneeling position, shoulder butt for firing in the prone position, cheek protector and carrying handle and strap.

Above: *The Armbrust 300 Anti-Tank Weapon.*

Panzerfaust 44 Anti-Tank Weapon — Germany(FGR)

Calibre: 44mm
Weight: 7.8kg
Length: 88cm(unloaded)
118cm(loaded)
Range: 200m(old round)
400m(new round)
Crew: 1

The PZF.44 is the standard light anti-tank weapon of the German Army and is believed to be in service with a number of other NATO countries. It is of the re-useable type and can be quickly re-loaded. The original round has been replaced by a new round which has been developed by Dynamit Nobel AG. Basic data of the two rounds is given below:

	Old Round	New Round
Calibre of rocket	81mm	67mm
Initial velocity	107m/s	168m/s
Maximum velocity	107m/s	210m/s
Maximum range	200m	400m
Armour penetration	320mm	370mm

.38 No 2 Pistol Revolver — Great Britain

Calibre: 0.38in(9.65mm)
Length: 26cm
Length of Barrel: 12.7cm
Weight: 0.767kg
Cylinder Capacity: 6 rounds
Muzzle Velocity: 183m/s
Maximum Effective Range: 30m

Developed from the earlier .38in Webley Mark IV pistol, the .38in No 2 Pistol Revolver is often referred to as the 'Enfield'. It is no longer in service with the British forces but is still used by many UK police forces and remains in service in New Zealand, Cyprus, and many other Commonwealth and ex-Commonwealth armies and police forces. There are two main versions, the No 2 Mark 1, and the No 2 Mark 1* which has a double-action only trigger mechanism and thus lacks a hammer thumb notch.

Top right: *The .38 No 2 revolver.*

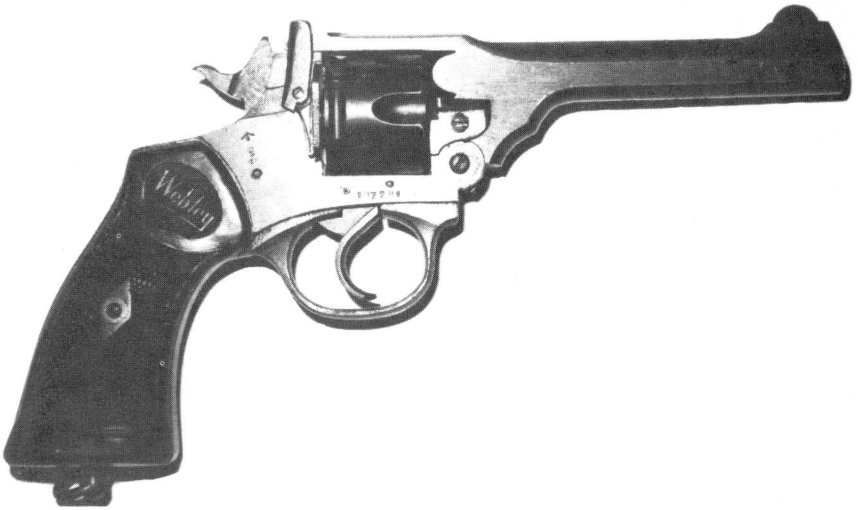

.455 Webley Pistol

Great Britain

Calibre(Nominal): 0.455in(11.6mm)
Calibre(Actual): 0.441in(11.2mm)
Length: 28.6cm
Length of Barrel: 15.2cm
Weight Empty: 1.07kg
Cylinder Capacity: 6 rounds
Muzzle Velocity: 183m/s
Maximum Effective Range: 50m

The first Webley 0.455 pistol entered service in 1887 and since that time has been produced in large numbers in a variety of marks and with different barrel lengths. The last service mark was the Pistol, Webley, 6-in barrel, Mark 6 which entered service in 1915 and it was declared obsolete by the British Army in 1947 by which time it was known as the Pistol Revolver .455 No 1 Mark 6. Despite its age it is still in use all over the world as its massive and heavy construction ensures that it will take a long time to wear out and the large calibre bullet is very useful for close-quarter fighting. The Webley .455 is still likely to be encountered in such countries as Egypt and Jordan, and it remains in service with many British-trained armies and police forces.

Below: *The .455 Webley Pistol.*

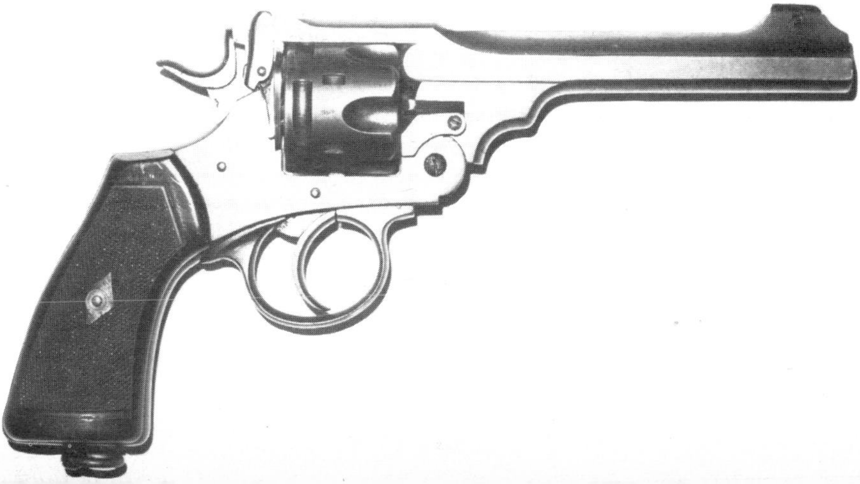

Sterling Sub-Machine Gun 9mm Mark 4 (L2A3)

Great Britain

Calibre: 9mm
Length—Butt Folded: 48.2cm
Length—Butt Extended: 69cm
Length of Barrel: 19.8cm
Weight Loaded: 3.47kg
Magazine Capacity: 34 rounds
Muzzle Velocity: 390m/s
Range: 200m
Rate of Fire: 550rpm(cyclic)

Adopted for British Forces use in 1954 (as the L3A4) the Sterling has been sold to well over seventy military and defence forces throughout the world. Developed from the earlier Patchett smg, the Sterling can be fitted with a bayonet and it is a reliable and efficient weapon under a wide range of conditions. Single-shot fire can be selected, and the sights have two range settings—100m and 200m. This weapon is also manufactured in Canada (as the C1) and in India.

Below: *The Sterling SMG with butt folded.*
Bottom: *The Sterling SMG with bayonet and with butt extended.*

Sterling Patchett Silenced Sub-Machine Gun 9mm Mark 5 (L34A1)

Great Britain

Calibre: 9mm
Length—Butt Folded: 65.4cm
Length—Butt Extended: 85.7cm
Length of Barrel: 19.8cm
Weight Loaded: 4.25kg
Magazine Capacity: 34 rounds
Muzzle Velocity: 308m/s
Range—Maximum Effective: 150m
Rate of Fire: 515–565rpm(cyclic)
102rpm(practical)

The Mark 5 Sterling was designed to a British General Staff specification which called for a weapon that when fired would be inaudible at 30m and unrecognisable as a firearm when fired at a range of 50m. The Mark 5 is basically a Sterling Mark 4 with an advanced design of silencer added and mechanically the two Marks are identical. In use the weapon would be fired using aimed single shots only, with the automatic fire mode being used only as an emergency extra. The Scotos night sight can be fitted as an extra.

Above: *The Sterling Patchett SMG Mark 5(L34A1) with stock folded.*

Below: *The Sterling Patchett SMG 5(L34A1) with stock extended.*

The Sten Guns

Great Britain

(Mark 11)
Calibre: 9mm
Length: 76.2cm
Length of Barrel: 19.7cm
Weight Unloaded: 2.8kg
Weight Loaded: 3.44kg
Magazine Capacity: 32 rounds
Muzzle Velocity: 366m/s
Maximum Effective Range: 200m
Rate of Fire: 540rpm

The Sten was first produced in 1940 and was designed for easy manufacture at low cost. It was produced in a variety of Marks, the most numerous of which was the Mark 11 and over 2 000 000 were made. Other Marks featured silencers and such extras as wooden butts and foregrips. Although now withdrawn from use in most front-line forces throughout the world, the Sten is still in use with some police forces and military units, both regular and irregular.

Below: *The 9mm Sten Sub-Machine Gun.*

7.62mm Rifle L42A1

Great Britain

Calibre: 7.62mm
Length: 118.1cm
Length of Barrel: 69.9cm
Weight: 4.43kg
Magazine Capacity: 10 rounds
Muzzle Velocity: 838m/s
Range: 800–1 000m

The L42A1 is a version of the 7.62mm L39A1 intended for service use by snipers. (The L39A1 is not intended primarily as a service rifle but is intended for competition use by Army units, and differs from the L49A1 in many details). Basically, the L49A1 is a conversion of the No 4 Mark 1(T) rifles to take 7.62mm ammunition. A L1A1 sighting telescope is fitted as standard, but fixed sights are still incorporated.

Below: *The 7.62mm L42A1 Sniper's Rifle with telescopic sight.*

Rifle No 5 Mark 1

Great Britain

Calibre: .303in(7.7mm)
Length: 100.3cm
Length of Barrel: 47.6cm
Weight: 3.24kg
Magazine Capacity: 10 rounds
Range—Maximum Effective: 400m

Designed in 1943 the No 5 Mark 1 was a shortened version of the No 4 intended for use in the jungles of the Far East. It was fitted with a flash hider and as recoil was rather heavy a rubber butt pad was also standard. Now out of service with British forces the No 5 remains in use with some Asian states.

Bottom left: *The Rifle No. 5 Mk. 1 which was designed for use in the Far East.*

Rifle No 4 Mark 1

Great Britain

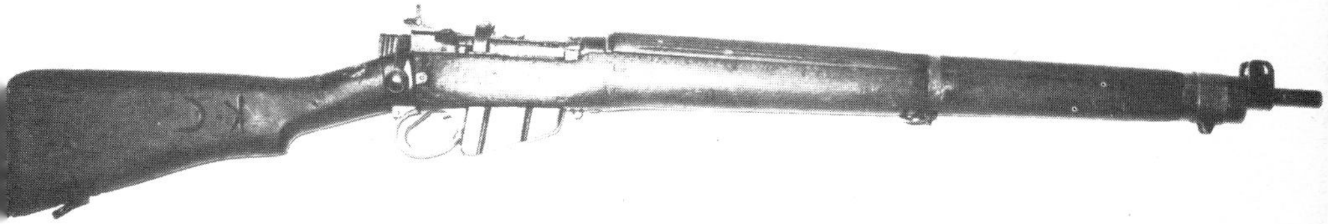

Calibre: .303in(7.7mm)
Length: 112.85cm
Length of Barrel: 64cm
Weight: 4kg
Magazine Capacity: 10 rounds
Muzzle Velocity: 751ft/sec
Range: Sighted up to 1 300 yd(1 280m)

The No 4 Mark 1 was approved for production in November, 1939 after trials had taken place as far back as 1926. The new rifle was designed for mass production and differed from the earlier No 1 rifles in having part of the barrel protruding from the front of stock. The sights and trigger mechanism were also revised. The No 4 was produced in millions in the UK and in Canada, the USA and India. After extensive use during World War 2 and since, the No 4 is no longer in front-line service with British Forces but it remains in use with some TAVR units and the Ulster Defence Regiment. Overseas it is still in front-line use with Middle East and Asian armies, and large numbers have been converted for sporting purposes. The No 4 can be fitted with a spike or blade bayonet, and is also used to fire a variety of grenades. There are a number of sub-variants such as the No 4 Mark 1*, the Mark 2, the Mark 1/2 and 1/3, none of which differ from the original Mark except in minor manufacturing detail.

The No 4 Mark 1 rifle is still regarded as one of the finest military rifles ever produced.

Some No 4 Mark 1 rifles have been rebored to the standard 7.62mm calibre and in this form are known as the L8A4. Both these and the .303 versions can be fitted with telescopic sights (eg Rifle No 4 Mark 1(T) and Mark 1*(T)).

Above: *The Rifle No 4 Mark 1.*

Rifle No 1 SMLE Mark 111*

Great Britain

Calibre: .303in(7.7mm)
Length: 113cm
Length of Barrel: 64cm
Weight: 3.91kg
Magazine Capacity: 10 rounds
Muzzle Velocity: 744m/s
Range—Effective: Up to 1 000m

The Rifle No 1 Mark 111* was first manufactured in 1916 and was a simplified version of the No 1 Mark 111. To ease production the Mark 111* did not have a magazine cut-off and the sights were simpler. The Mark 111* was produced in large quantities both in the UK and India, and the Mark 111* remained in production in Australia until 1955 (the Australian Army did not adopt the later No 4 rifle). Over the years the No 1 Mark 111* was produced with some minor variations and as the type was essentially a hand-built weapon, some variations on the above dimensions may occur. In 1975 the Mark 111* is still in widespread use in the Middle East and India and its robust and reliable construction will ensure a long life for it yet.

Below: *The Rifle No 1 SMLE Mark 111**.*

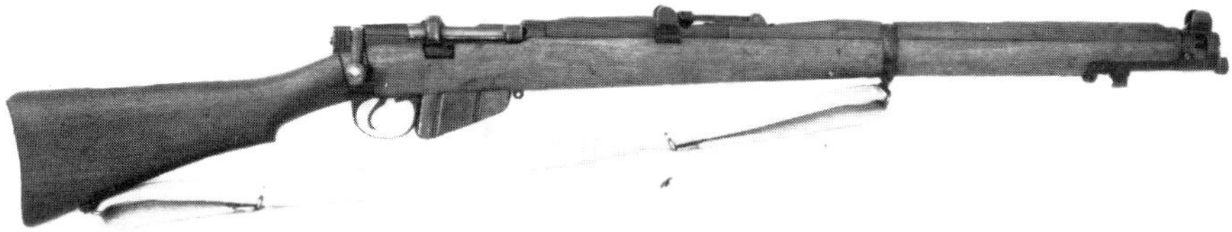

7.62mm Light Machine Gun L4A4 — Great Britain

Calibre: 7.62mm
Length: 113.3cm
Length of Barrel: 53.6cm
Weight of Gun: 9.5kg
Magazine Capacity: 20 or 30 rounds
Muzzle Velocity: 823m/s
Range—Maximum Effective: 800m
Rate of Fire: 500rpm(cyclic)

The L4A4 is a conversion of the WW2 .303 Bren Gun and so many conversions have been made over the years that it is very unlikely that any .303 Bren Guns remain in use anywhere (some 7.92mm versions produced in Canada during WW2 may be encountered in the Far East, especially in China). Despite the 7.62mm conversion, the basic gas-operated mechanism of the Czech-designed Bren remains unchanged. Although no longer in front-line use with the British Army the L4A4 equips many units of the TAVR and is fitted to many vehicles as an AA weapon. Overseas, the L4A4 is in use in Australia and Malaysia, and in many other Commonwealth countries.

The L4A5 is a variant used by the Royal Navy.

Top right: *The 7.62mm Light Machine Gun L4A4.*
Below: *The standard .303 Bren Light Machine Gun.*

7.62mm General Purpose Machine Gun L7A2

Great Britain

Calibre: 7.62mm
Length as LMG: 123.2cm
Length of Barrel: 62.8cm
Weight: 10.9kg
Weight of L4A1 Tripod: 13.64kg
Type of Feed: 100 rounds in linked belt
Muzzle Velocity: 838m/s
Range: Up to 1 800m
Rate of Fire: 750–1 000rpm(cyclic)
LMG—up to 100rpm
Sustained fire on tripod—up to 200rpm

The L7A2 is the version of the Belgian FN MAG machine gun adopted for use by the British Army and it differs from the original in several respects. Most of these changes have been designed in at Enfield and outwardly the gun is identical with the Belgian MAG. The L7A2 is usually known as the GPMG and it can be used as a LMG on a bipod or as a sustained fire weapon on a tripod. In this latter role a dial sight (the same as that used on the 81mm mortar) can be used for indirect firing.

Below: *GPMG for use in the sustained fire role with tripod and dial sight*

The L8A1 is a variant designed for use on the Chieftain tank and a further variant is the L43A1 intended for use on the Scorpion light tank as a ranging machine gun. The L8A1 is designed for use as a normal MG for ground use as is the L37A1 fitted to a variety of light AFVs.

The L20A1 is a variant for use on helicopters and aircraft machine gun pods.

Above: *The GPMG being carried by a private of the 4th Battalion (V) The Parachute Rgt.*

Vickers Machine Gun

Great Britain

Calibre: .303in(7.7mm)
Length: 115.6cm
Length of Barrel: 72.4cm
Weight Without Water: 15kg
Weight With Water: 18.2kg
Weight of Tripod: 22.7kg
Type of Feed: 250-round belts
Muzzle Velocity: 744m/s
Maximum Range(Mark 8Z round): 4 117m
Rate of Fire: 450–500rpm

The Vickers machine gun was a development of the basic Maxim machine gun introduced into service as the Mark 1 in 1912. Despite the introduction of various Marks for such uses as AFV installations, the basic design remained unchanged until its withdrawal from service with the British Army in 1968. However, it remains in service with some Middle and Far East forces (eg Arab Emirates and Pakistan) where its rugged and reliable construction continues to be appreciated. Its main disadvantage is its great weight, but with the Mark 8Z round it can be used at ranges of up to 4 117m and is fitted with a dial sight for indirect fire.

Below: *The Vickers .303 in Mk 1 Machine Gun complete with ammunition box and can for cooling water.*

51mm Mortar

Great Britain

Calibre: 51mm
Length: 51.5cm
Weight Complete: 4.6kg
Maximum Range: 800m
Minimum Range: 200m
Bomb Weight(HE): 0.852kg

The 51mm Mortar has been designed to replace the elderly 2-inch Mortar (cf) in service with the British Army and is a simple weapon with a minimum of design complexities. The sight is a bubble device and elevation is altered by a telescopic monopod leg. For minimum ranges an insert with a long firing pin is fitted inside the barrel to shorten its effective length. The HE bomb is of advanced design and is constructed with a number of pre-formed fragments around the HE filling.

ML 2-in Mortar

Great Britain

(Marks 7* and 8)

Calibre: 2.015in(51.18mm)
Length Complete: 35.6cm
Weight Complete: 3.3kg
Maximum Range: 500m
Bomb Weight(HE): 1.022kg
Bomb Weight(Smoke): 0.909kg
Bomb Weight(Signal): 0.511kg

The 2-in Mortar originated before WW2 and since 1945 has been used only for smoke and signal firing (the HE round was re-introduced for a short time during the Borneo campaign). Although it was produced in a wide range of marks and submarks only the Marks 7* and 8, both with spade baseplates, remain in use. Sighting for both is a simple white line painted on the barrel. The 2-in Mortar is due for replacement by the 51mm Mortar is the near future.

The 2-in Mortar remains in service in Pakistan and Denmark (as the 51mm Mortar M/45 Fa).

Above: *The ML 2-In Mortar in action.*

4.85mm Individual Weapon

Great Britain

Calibre: 4.85mm
Length: 77cm
Length of Barrel: 51.85cm
Weight(Loaded): 4.12kg
Magazine Capacity: 20 rounds
Muzzle Velocity: 900m/s
Rate of Fire: 700-850rpm(cyclic)

The British submission for a new standard NATO calibre has been under development since about 1970, and the resultant calibre selection of 4.85mm (0.191in) has been arrived at after a long series of trials. The weapon to fire the new round, the 4.85mm Individual Weapon has been developed by the Royal Small Arms Factory, Enfield. This weapon is fitted with an advanced optical sight, a small bayonet and can fire grenades. A night sight is under development. The Individual Weapon is conventionally gas-operated and uses a rotary forward locking bolt. Weight of a 4.85mm round is 11.6 grams.

Bottom left: *The new personal 4.8mm weapon with its distinctive optical sight is made even more unusual by its lack of orthodox butt which allows the weapon to use a barrel of suitable length while being much shorter over all.*

4.85mm Light Support Weapon — Great Britain

Calibre: 4.85mm
Length: 90cm
Length of Barrel: 64.6cm
Weight(Loaded): 5.26kg
Magazine Capacity: 20 or 30 rounds
Muzzle Velocity: 930m/s
Rate of Fire: 700-850rpm(cyclic)

Developed by the Royal Small Arms Factory, Enfield, the Light Support Weapon (LSW) uses 80% of the components used on the Individual Weapon. The main changes are to the barrel, which is longer and a bipod is a permanent fixture. Normally a thirty round magazine is used but the Individual Weapon's twenty-round magazine can also be used. Considerably lighter than the 7.62mm GPMG it is intended to replace, the LSW will probably be issued to infantry units at the rate of one LSW to every three Individual Weapons.

Above: *The 4.85mm infantry machine gun, properly known as the Light Support Weapon, is very similar to the personal weapon and shares many of its components. The obvious exterior differences are the longer barrel, larger magazines and bipod.*

Sterling 5.56mm AR-18 BP Light Rifle — Great Britain

The Sterling Armament Company have taken up licence production of the American AR-18 and AR-18S in preference to their own Light Automatic Rifle which was not taken beyond the prototype stage. Sterlings have continued their own development work on the basic AR-18 and in June 1976 first showed publicly a drastically revised variant, the AR-18 BP (BP = bull-pup). This light rifle uses AR-18 parts rearranged so that the trigger mechanism is in front of the receiver. In this form the AR-18 BP is being directed towards police forces who would find this bull-pup configuration light and handy. A twenty-round magazine is used as standard. No further data is available.

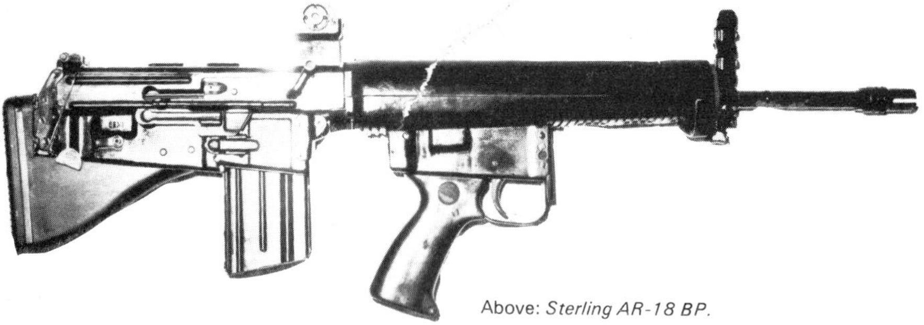

Above: *Sterling AR-18 BP.*

Sterling 5.56mm AR-18 Light Machine Gun

As well as producing the AR-18 in a bull-pup configuration, Sterlings have also developed a light machine gun version of the same weapon family. The basic AR-18 has been altered to take an easily removed barrel housed in a light steel barrel jacket and fitted with a light bipod. The basic AR-18 receiver and mechanism remain unchanged, and a variety of different sighting systems can be used. Twenty or thirty-round magazines can be fitted. This AR-18 variant was first shown publicly in June 1976. No further data is available.

Below: *Sterling AR-18 Light Machine Gun.*

9mm Pistol PA-63

Hungary

Calibre: 9mm
Length: 17.5cm
Length of Barrel: 8.9cm
Weight: .665kg(loaded)
.597kg(empty)
Magazine Capacity: 7 rounds
Range: 50m

The PA-63 is a commercial weapon and may well be used by the Hungarian Armed Forces. It fires a 9mm cartridge with a m/v of 315m/s.

Other Hungarian Pistols
The 7.62mm Model 48 is essentially a copy of the German Walther PP pistol and is used by the

Hungarian Police. It is a double-action blowback-operated weapon.

The 9mm Walam 48 is not used by the Hungarian Armed Forces.

7.62mm Model 48(48M) is the Hungarian model of the Soviet TT-33 pistol. It differs from the Soviet weapon in that is has vertical cuts on its slide, its grip markings consist of a star, wheatsheaf and a hammer, surrounded by a wreath. A 9mm model of the TT-33 has been built but this is not used in Hungary.

7.62mm AMD Sub-Machine Gun — Hungary

Calibre: 7.62mm
Length: 85.1cm(butt extended)
64.8cm(butt folded)
Length of Barrel: 31.8cm
Weight: 3.27kg
Magazine Capacity: 30 rounds
Muzzle Velocity: 700m/s
Range: 300m
Rate of Fire: 600rpm(cyclic)
120rpm(automatic)
40rpm(single shots)

The Hungarian AMD is a sub-machine gun based on the standard AKM Assault Rifle. It has the same breech mechanism but a shorter barrel, forward pistol grip and a large muzzle brake. The rear sight is graduated to 800m rather than the 1 000m of standard AKM's. The stock folds along the right side of the weapon when not required. The AMD cannot be fitted with a bayonet. It fires the same 7.62mm × 39 cartridge as the AKM but with a slightly lower muzzle velocity.

Below: *The 7.62mm AMD SMG with stock extended.*

9mm UZI Sub-Machine Gun — Israel

Calibre: 9mm
Length—Wood Stock: 64cm
Length—Metal Stock Extended: 64cm
Length—Metal Stock Folded: 47cm
Length of Barrel: 25.9cm
Weight with Empty Magazine: 3.6kg
Weight Loaded: 4.13kg
Magazine Capacity: 25, 32 or 64 rounds
Muzzle Velocity: 400m/s
Maximum Effective Range: 200m
Rate of Fire: 550-600rpm(cyclic)
128rpm(automatic)
64rpm(single shot)

The Uzu sub-machine gun was designed in 1949 by Major Uzi Gal of the Israeli Army and it embodies a number of features taken from experimental Czech and other designs to form a very useful and sturdy weapon. One of the main design features of the Uzi is its short length brought about by the use of a bolt that extends forward over the barrel, and the magazine housing is in the pistol grip. The gun is fired as the bolt travels forward so that the blowback bolt is lighter than the conventional equivalent. Manufacture has been simplified by the use of metal stampings and heat-resistant plastics. One useful feature for the soldier is that the magazines have viewing holes in their sides so that the magazine contents can be seen at a glance. The stock can be easily changed from a conventional wooden butt to a folding metal stock and a number of other accessories can be fitted. These include a bayonet, searchlight, grenade launcher and blank firing device. A special clip is used to join two magazines together in a 'L' configuration. The Uzi is manufactured by Israeli Military Industries for the Israeli

Army and is licence-built by the Belgian FN concern for the Bundeswehr, where it is used as the MP-2. Other user nations are Iran, Venezuala and Thailand.

Below: *The 9mm UZI Sub-Machine Gun with conventional wooden butt.*

Above: *The 9mm UZI Sub-Machine Gun with folding metal stock.*

5.56mm Galil ARM Assault Rifle Israel

Calibre: 5.56mm
Length—Stock Extended: 97cm (82cm)
Length—Stock Folded: 74cm (60cm)
Length of Barrel: 46cm (33cm)
Weight with Bipod and Handle: 4.3kg
Weight—Basic: 3.9kg (3.5kg)
Weight Loaded–35 rounds: 5.01kg (4.21kg)
Magazine Capacity: 12, 35 or 50 rounds
Muzzle Velocity: 980m/s (920m/s)
Maximum Effective Range: 600m (400m)
Rate of Fire: 650rpm(cyclic)
105rpm(automatic)
40rpm(single shot)

(Data in brackets refers to Galil SAR)

After the 1967 Six-Day War a series of trials were carried out by the Israeli Army to find an infantry weapon that could replace its existing range of rifles, sub-machine guns and light machine guns. In 1972 it chose the Galil assault rifle and production began in time for the first examples to be issued in 1974 and 1975. The Galil is an Israeli product based on the Finnish M62 which in its turn is a derivation of the Russian AK-47 assault rifle. As produced, the Galil has several unusual features not the least of which is the fixed bipod that can be used as a wire-cutter. The operating handle, fire-selector and magazine catch can be used from either side of the weapon to ease handling by left and right-handed people. As well as the standard Galil rifle there is a shorter version, the Galil SAR (short assault rifle) which has no bipod but can be fitted with an optional fore-grip. Both versions can be fitted with a bayonet, a plastic or wooden stock, blank firing attachment and both can be fitted with the 12-round magazine loaded with ballistite cartridges for firing grenades.

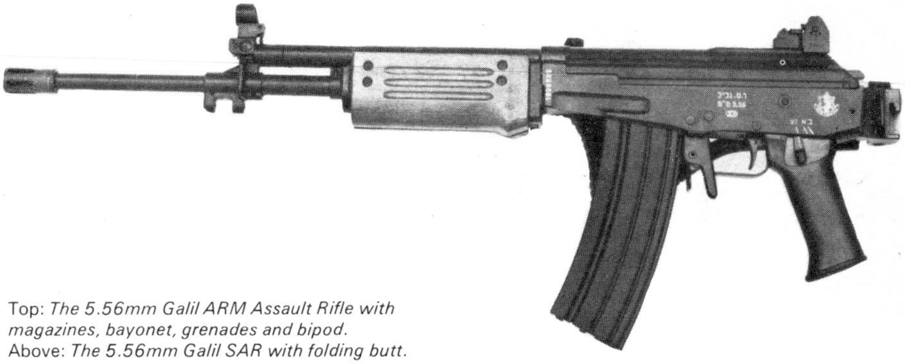

Top: *The 5.56mm Galil ARM Assault Rifle with magazines, bayonet, grenades and bipod.*
Above: *The 5.56mm Galil SAR with folding butt.*

52mm Mortar

Israel

Calibre: 52mm
Total Weight: 7.9kg(with base plate)
1.31kg(bipod only)
Overall Length: 63.7cm
Length of Barrel: 49cm
Range: 130m(minimum)
480m(maximum)
Crew: 2

This 52mm smooth-bore muzzle loaded mortar is manufactured by Israel Military Industries. The gunner holds the mortar with the baseplate on the ground and uses the white sight line on the barrel for aiming. The mortar is fired by turning the firing button at the base of the barrel. This weapon is employed by infantry units for plunging fire as well as direct fire from the prone position.

Three types of mortar bomb have been developed by Israel Military Industries for this weapon:

HE Round: Total weight is 1.02kg and it has a length of 250mm, main charge is 150g of TNT. M/v is 78m/s, maximum range of 460–480m at 45° angle of fire. Fitted with IMI No. 161 fuse.
Smoke Round: Total weight is .92kg, 240mm long. Maximum range 400m, m/v 78m/s, smoke generates for approx 100 seconds. Time delay is 7.5 seconds.
Illuminating Round: Total weight is .8kg, length 260mm. The parachute opens after 8 seconds at 350m range and a height of 100m. Illuminating power is 100 000 candelas, burns for approx. 30 seconds.

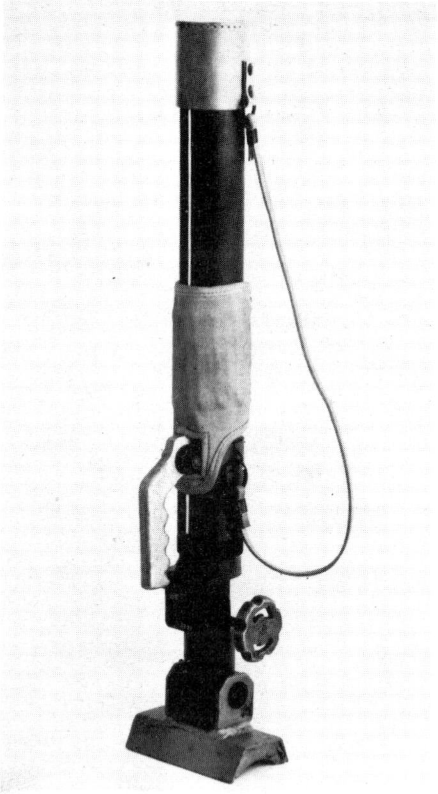

Left: *The IMI 52mm Mortar.*

60mm Tampella Mortar

Israel

Calibre: 60.75mm
Total Weight: 14.5kg
5.5kg(barrel and breech piece)
1.1kg(sight)
4.3kg(bipod)
3.4kg(baseplate)
Length of Barrel: 74cm
Elevation: +40° to +79°
Traverse: 116° at 50° elevation
137° at 70° elevation
Range: 150m(minimum)
2 555m(maximum)
Crew: 2(1 man can carry the complete weapon)

This smooth-bore muzzle-loaded weapon is manufactured by Soltam and can be used with or without the bipod. The barrel and breech are made of high tensile alloy steel. The baseplate is of welded construction and carries the breech piece ball socket

Right: *The 60mm Tampella Mortar.*

in the centre. The bipod incorporates the elevating, traverse and divergence gear and is made of seamless steel tubes.

HE Bomb: Forged steel construction with a tail unit machined out of a piece of a single of extruded light metal. The charge system is so arranged that secondaries cannot be ignited in a hot barrel. Weight is 1.541kg. The propellant system is made up of a primary charge and a combination of up to 4 secondary charges.

Smoke Bomb: Weight 1.541kg. ballistic and propelling charges same as the HE bomb. Used both as a smoke bomb and as a ranging bomb and is filled with plastic phosphorus.

Beretta 9mm Model 1951 Pistol — Italy

Calibre: 9mm
Length: 20.3cm
Length of Barrel: 11.4cm
Weight: .89kg(empty-steel receiver)
.72kg(empty-aluminium receiver)
Magazine Capacity: 8 or 10 rounds(latter being a special magazine)
Range: 50m
Rate of Fire: 35rpm

The Beretta 9mm Model 1951 pistol is the standard pistol of the Italian Armed Forces and is also used by both Egypt and Israel. It is short recoil-operated and semi-automatic. It fires standard 9mm × 19 parabellum ammunition with a m/v of 350m/s. The foresight is of the blade type and the rearsight of notch type.

Above: *The Beretta 9mm Model 1951 Pistol.*

Beretta Model 1934 9mm (Short) Pistol — Italy

Calibre: 9mm
Length: 15.2cm
Length of Barrel: 8.9cm
Weight: .763kg(with loaded magazine)
.697kg(with empty magazine)
Magazine Capacity: 7
Range: 40m
Rate of Fire: 28rpm

The Model 1934 is a development of an earlier Beretta design and is used by the Italian and Yugoslav Armies. It fires a short 9mm round with a m/v of 290m/s. It is blowback operated and semi-automatic. The foresight is of the blade type and the rear sight is of the notch type.

Above: *The Beretta Model 1934 9mm(Short) Pistol.*

Beretta 9mm Sub-Machine Gun Model 12 Italy

Calibre: 9mm
Length: 64.5cm with steel butt extended
41.8cm with steel butt folded
Length of Barrel: 20cm
Weight: 3.4kg(wooden butt without magazine)
3kg(steel butt without magazine)
Magazine Capacity: 20, 30 or 40 rounds
Range: 200m(effective)
Rate of Fire: 550rpm(cyclic)
120rpm(automatic)
40rpm(single shots)

In the 1950's Beretta developed a number of SMG's as successors to the earlier MAB 38/49. The end result was the Model 12 which has been exported to a number of countries and has been built in Indonesia. Although some are used by special units of the Italian Army, their standard SMG remains the MAB 38/39.

System of operation is blowback and it fires standard 9mm parabellum ammunition. The foresight is of the blade type and the rearsight is of the flip type graduated for 100 and 200m.

It can fire either single shots or on full automatic, the selector being of the push through type. It is available with either a wooden detachable butt or a steel folding butt.

Top right: *The Beretta 9mm Sub-Machine Gun Model 12 with steel folding butt.*

Beretta 9mm Sub-Machine Gun Model 38/49 (Model 4)

Italy

Calibre: 9mm
Length: 79cm
Length of Barrel: 21cm
Weight: 4.64kg
3.89kg(without magazine)
Magazine Capacity: 20 or 40 rounds
Range: 200m(maximum effective)
Rate of Fire: 450/500rpm(cyclic)
120rpm(automatic)
40rpm(single shots)

The Beretta MAB 38/49(MAB = Moschetto Automatico Beretta) is a development of the earlier Model 38/44. The Model 4 has a manual safety catch whilst the Model 5 has an automatic safety catch. The front sight is of the blade type and the rear sight is of the U-notch type and set for 100m. The weapon has two triggers, the front one for single shots and the rear one for full automatic. It fires standard 9mm parabellum ammunition.

The Model 38/49 (Models 4 and 5) is th standard SMG of the Italian Army and has been exported all over the world. It has also been built in Indonesia and a similar weapon is the San Cristobal SMG.

Below: *The 9mm Beretta SMG Model 38/49 (Model 4).*

Beretta 9mm Sub-Machine Gun Model M38/42 — Italy

Four models were developed and used during the World War 2 and some of these remain in service today, for example in Romania and Yugoslavia. The M38/42 and M38/44 have no barrel jacket but use a lighter externally fluted barrel, their stock ending at the magazine. On the M38 and M38A however the stock ends half way down the barrel.

Beretta Model 70 5.56mm Rifle Family — Italy

	AR	SC	LMG
Calibre:	5.56mm	5.56mm	5.56mm
Length with Bayonet:	108cm	107.5cm	108cm
Length W/O Bayonet:	94cm	93.5cm	94cm
Length of Barrel:	45cm	45cm	45cm
Weight(W/O Mag and Bayonet):	3.43kg	3.54kg	4.05kg
Magazine Capacity:	30 rounds	30 rounds	30 rounds
Effective Range:	500m	400m	500m
Rate of Fire(Cyclic):	630rpm	630rpm	600rpm
Rate of Fire(Automatic):	100rpm	100rpm	100rpm
Rate of Fire(single shots):	40rpm	40rpm	40rpm

There are three basic weapons in this Beretta rifle family:

1. AR Assault Rifle with a detachable rigid stock
2. SC Special Carbine with a detachable folding stock
3. LMG with a heavy barrel, carrying handle, bipod and a rigid stock.

Their system of operation is rotating bolt, gas-operated, they fire the 5.56mm × 45 cartridge with a m/v of 970m/s and fire either full automatic or single shots. They are provided with a grenade launcher (for 40mm Mecar grenades) which also acts as a flash suppressor, the grenade launching sight is a part of the aperture sight assembly. Accessories include a bayonet, telescopic sight sling and bipod.

Recently Beretta have developed a short version of the Special Carbine, this has been designed for the use of infantry mounted in MICV's and the weapon can be used through firing ports.

The Malaysian Army has purchased a large number of the Assault Rifle model.

Above: *Beretta Special Carbine and* below *the short model of the Special Carbine.*

7.62mm Beretta BM 59 Rifle — Italy

Calibre: 7.62mm
Length: 123.5cm(with bayonet)
109.5cm(without bayonet)
Length of Barrel: 49.1cm
Weight: 5.65kg(with loaded magazine, bayonet and sling)
4.4kg(without accessories)
Magazine Capacity: 20 rounds
Range: 600m
Rate of Fire: 800rpm(cyclic)
120rpm(automatic)
40rpm(single shots)

Note: Above data relates to the BM 59 ITAL

After the end of the World War 2 Beretta built large numbers of the American M1 Garland Rifle and the BM 59 is a development of this but chambered for the 7.62mm × 51 NATO cartridge. Various models have been developed: Mk. 1 when fitted with a bipod is the standard Italian Army rifle and is known as the BM 59 ITAL; Mk.2 has a pistol grip, and a bipod; Mk.3 has two pistol grips and a folding metal stock. The ITAL TA is used by the Italian Alpini troops whilst the ITAL Para is used by Italian Parachute units. The Mk.4 has a heavy barrel and is used as a LMG.

The BM 59 can fire either single shots or full automatic and can also fire anti-personnel and anti-tank grenades.

Below: *The Beretta BM 59 Mark ITAL.*
Bottom: *The Beretta BM 59 Mark ITAL Alpini.*

Folgore Anti-Tank Weapon

Italy

Calibre: 80mm
Length: 150cm
Weight: 10.8kg(launcher only)
Maximum Range: 500–700m
Minimum Range: 50–75m
Crew: 1–2

The Folgore anti-tank weapon has been developed by Breda Meccanica Bresciana with the assistance of Snia Viscosa. It is now in its final stages of development but is not yet in production.

The weapon is provided with an optical sight, stabilising leg and a carrying handle. The projectile is fin-stabilised and rocket-assisted, weighs 4.8kg, is 60cm in length, muzzle velocity is 650m/s.

Below: *A Folgore Anti-Tank Weapon in the field.*

9mm SCK Sub-Machine Gun

Japan

Calibre: 9mm
Length—Stock Extended: 76.2cm
Length—Stock Folded: 50.2cm
Weight: 3.35kg
Magazine Capacity: 30 rounds
Muzzle Velocity: 381m/s
Maximum Effective Range: 200m
Rate of Fire: 600rpm(cyclic)

Produced by the Shin Choo Kogyo KK, Tokyo, the SCK was first manufactured in 1960, and it now equips many Japanese Self Defence Force units. The design has features taken from the American M3A1, the Danish Madsen and the British Sten, and uses a conventional blowback mechanism.

7.62mm Type 64 Rifle

Japan

Calibre: 7.62mm
Length: 99cm
Length of Barrel: 45cm
Weight: 4.3kg(with bipod but without magazine)
.487kg(loaded magazine)
Magazine Capacity: 20 rounds
Muzzle Velocity: 700m/s(reduced charge)
800m/s(full charge)
Range: 400m
Rate of Fire: 470rpm(cyclic)
100rpm(rapid fire)
20rpm(sustained)

The Type 64 is the standard rifle of the Japanese Self Defence Force and was designed and built by the Howa Machinery Company Limited.

The weapon fires a standard 7.62mm × 51 NATO cartridge but with a reduced charge to suit the stature of the Japanese soldier. The gas regulator can be adjusted to launch rifle grenades or for full charge cartridges. It is gas-operated and the method of locking is of the tilting block type.

The foresight is of the blade type and the rearsight is of the aperture type and graduated for 200 and 400m. A bipod is provided.

7.62mm Type 62 Machine Gun — Japan

Calibre: 7.62mm
Length: 120cm
Length of Barrel: 63.5cm
Weight: 10.7kg
Muzzle Velocity: 855m/s
Range: 600m(bipod)
1100m(tripod)

The Type 62 Machine Gun was designed by the Nittoku Metal Industry Company and is the standard machine gun of the Japanese Self Defence Force. It entered service in 1962.

The weapon is gas-operated and fires the NATO 7.62mm × 51 cartridge and is fed from a disintegrating link belt. It is air-cooled, full automatic and has a quick change barrel. The foresight is of the blade type and the rear sight is of the leaf aperture type. A bipod is provided and the weapon can be mounted on a tripod for the sustained fire role if required and in this role the bipod is folded up underneath the barrel. A telescopic sight is also available.

9mm P-64 Pistol — Poland

Calibre: 9mm
Length: 15.5cm
Length of Barrel: 8.46cm
Weight Loaded: 0.68kg
Weight Empty: 0.636kg
Magazine Capacity: 6 rounds
Muzzle Velocity: 305m/s
Maximum Effective Range: 50m

The P-64 pistol has replaced the Soviet Pistolet TT in Polish Army service. It is conventional in design and has used some of the features of the Walther PP. It fires a 9mm × 18 cartridge. The P-64 uses a double action trigger and the safety catch is on the left. The weapon is issued complete with a holster, spare magazine and a cleaning rod.

9mm Machine Pistol PM-63 — Poland

Calibre: 9mm
Length—Stock Extended: 58.3cm
Length—Stock Folded: 33.3cm
Length of Barrel: 15cm
Weight Loaded—25 rounds: 1.8kg
Weight Empty: 1.55kg
Magazine Capacity: 15, 25 or 40 rounds
Muzzle Velocity: 320m/s
Maximum Effective Range: 200m—Stock Extended
40m without stock
Rate of Fire: 650rpm(cyclic)
75rpm(automatic)
40rpm(single shot)

The Pistolet Maszynowy PM-63 is also known as the Mini-Pistol and is similar in concept to the Czech Skorpion machine pistol. The PM-63 fires the 9mm × 18 Markarov round and is blowback operated. It is unusual in having no fire-selector as such as full or semi-automatic fire is achieved by trigger pressure. For accurate fire on full automatic a folding metal stock is fitted. A good recognition feature is the trough-like compensator above the muzzle which is supposed to keep the muzzle down on automatic fire. Each PM-63 is issued with a sling, hip holster, cleaning rod and four magazines. To date the PM-63 appears to have been used by parachute and crews of AFVs only.

Above: *The 9mm Machine Pistol PM-63.*

9mm FBP M.48 Sub-Machine Gun — Portugal

Calibre: 9mm
Length—Stock Extended: 81.3cm
Length—Stock Retracted: 63.5cm
Length of Barrel: 24.9cm
Weight Loaded: 4.43kg
Magazine Capacity: 32 rounds
Muzzle Velocity: 381m/s
Maximum Effective Range: 200m
Rate of Fire: 500rpm(cyclic)

This Portuguese design is a combination of a German MP40 bolt (with some changes) in a receiver based on that of the American M3 sub-machine gun. The M.48 is in service with the Portuguese Army and may therefore also be encountered in the parts of Africa where the Portuguese have been involved.

9mm M1941 (Orita) Sub-Machine Gun — Romania

Calibre: 9mm
Length: 89.4cm
Length of Barrel: 28.7cm
Weight Loaded: 4kg
Weight Empty: 3.45kg
Magazine Capacity: 25 or 32 rounds
Muzzle Velocity: 381m/s
Maximum Effective Range: 200m
Rate of Fire: 400rpm(cyclic)
120rpm(automatic)
50rpm(semi-automatic)

The Orita was built at the Cugir Arsenal in Rumania from 1941 to 1944. Although it is no longer in front-line service, it is still used by the Workers' Militia. There are two models—one has a folding metal stock rather like that used on the German MP40 and the other uses a conventional wooden stock. Construction is robust as all parts were machined from solid, a factor which no doubt explains the weapon's longevity. Operation is simple blowback, and one unusual feature is that the rear-sight is calibrated up to 500m.

9mm Makarov (PM) Pistol — Soviet Union

Calibre: 9mm
Length: 16cm
Barrel Length: 9.3cm
Weight: .81kg(with loaded magazine)
.73kg(with empty magazine)
.675kg(without magazine)
Magazine Capacity: 8 rounds
Range: 50m

The 9mm Makarov pistol was introduced into the Soviet Army after World War 2 and is very similiar in appearance to the Walther PP pistol. The Makarov is an eight-shot, blowback, magazine-fed pistol with a double-action trigger. This allows the hammer, if uncocked, to be cocked and released by a single long pull on the trigger. The weapon is also manufactured in East Germany and Communist China. The East German model is known as the Pistole M and has no lanyard loop and plain grips, the Soviet model was a star on

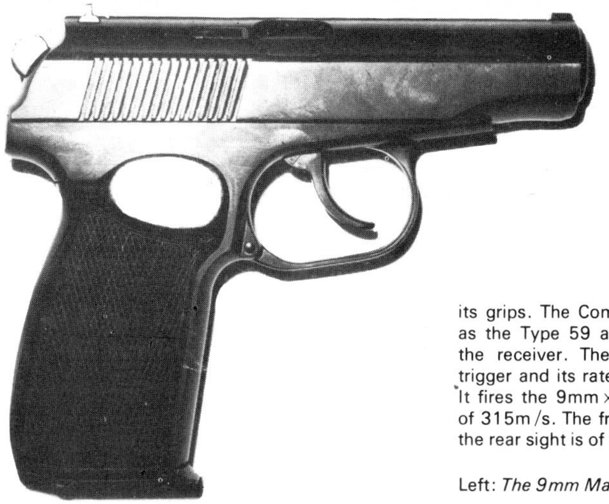

its grips. The Communist Chinese model is known as the Type 59 and has the markings 59 SHI on the receiver. The Makarov has a double action trigger and its rate of fire is 30 rounds per minute. It fires the 9mm × 18 cartridge, these have a m/v of 315m/s. The front sight is of the blade type and the rear sight is of the 'V' notch type.

Left: *The 9mm Makarov (PM) Pistol.*

9mm Stechkin (APS) Pistol

Soviet Union

Calibre: 9mm
Length with Stock: 54cm
Length of Pistol: 22.5cm
Barrel Length: 18.5cm
Weight: 1.78kg(with loaded magazine and holster)
1.22kg(with loaded magazine)
1.02kg(with empty magazine)
Magazine Capacity: 20 rounds
Range: 50m(practical)
150/200m(maximum with stock)

The 9mm Stechkin (APS) pistol was introduced after World War 2 and is now in very limited use. This weapon is a machine pistol as it has both semi-automatic (40rpm) or full automatic (90rpm) capability. The selector is on the left side of the receiver and has three positions—safe, semi-automatic and full automatic. To enable the weapon to be fired more accurately at longer ranges the wooden holster can be attached to the grip. The front sight is of the blade type and the rearsight is a V notch that can be adjusted for 25, 50,100 and 200m ranges. The weapon fires the same 9mm round with a m/v of 340m/s as the Makarov pistol. When being carried in the holster the grips of the Strechkin protrude.

Below: *The 9mm Strechkin (APS) Pistol.*

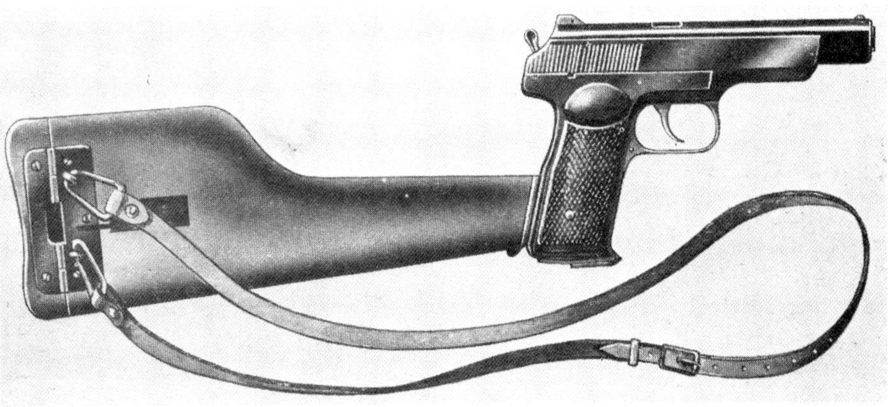

7.62mm Tula Tokarev M-1933 (or TT-33) Pistol

Soviet Union

Calibre: 7.62mm
Length: 19.5cm
Barrel Length: 11.6cm
Weight: .94kg(with loaded magazine)
.854kg(with empty magazine)
.769kg(without magazine)
Magazine Capacity: 8 rounds
Range: 45–50m

The TT-33 is based on a modified Colt-Browning design and has been replaced in the Soviet Army by the 9mm Marakov pistol. The TT-33 has been made in many countries including the following:

Soviet Union: With letters CCCP on the grips
Poland: With letters FB on the grips.
Hungary: This is known as the 48M and has also been made, in 9mm calibre. This model is known as the Tokagypt 58
Communist China: Two models—the Type 51 and Type 54
Yugoslavia: Known as the M-57
North Korea: Known as Type 68 and based on TT-33.

In most cases the foreign weapons differ in small details to the original Soviet weapon.

The TT-33 fires the 7.62mm × 25 Type P round which has a muzzle velocity of 420m/s. The weapon has no safety catch—the hammer is set at the half-cock position. The front sight is of the blade type and the rear is of the U-notch type.

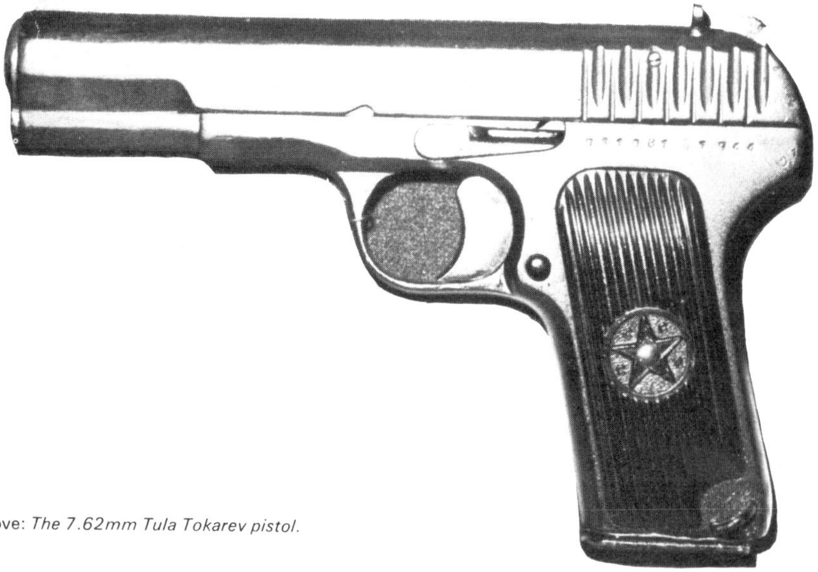

Above: *The 7.62mm Tula Tokarev pistol.*

7.62mm Sudayev M1943 Sub-Machine Gun (PPS)

Soviet Union

Calibre: 7.62mm
Length: 83.1cm(stock extended)
61.6cm(stock folded)
Length of Barrel: 27cm
Weight: 3.62kg(with loaded box magazine)
3.24kg(with empty box magazine)
3kg(without magazine)
Magazine Capacity: 35 rounds
Range: 200m(short bursts)
100m(long bursts)

The M1943(PPS) SMG was developed from the earlier PPS M1942 SMG during the early part of World War 2. The weapon is no longer in front line service with any of the Warsaw Pact Forces. It can only be operated as a full automatic although it is said that an experienced soldier can fire single rounds by touching the trigger in a certain way!

The PPS M1943 is of all-metal construction except for the grips which are of plastic. The metal shoulder stock can be folded along the top of the receiver when not required. The ejection port is on the right side of the receiver. The M1943 fires the

7.62mm × 25 cartridge which has a m/v of 500 m/s, cyclic rate of fire is 650rpm, practical rate of fire is 100rpm. The front sight is of the post type and the rearsight is of the L-type with a notch.

After World War 2 the Polish Army produced a model of this weapon with a number of modifications including a wooden stock and this was known as the M43/52. It has also been manufactured in Communist China as the Type 43 SMG.

Above: *The 7.62mm Sudayev M1943 Sub-Machine Gun (PPS).*

7.62mm Shpagin M1941 (PPSh) Sub-Machine Gun

Soviet Union

Calibre: 7.62mm
Length: 84.2cm
Length of Barrel: 27cm
Weight: 5.3kg(with loaded drum magazine)
4.1kg(with loaded box magazine)
4.6kg(with empty drum magazine)
3.78kg(with empty box magazine)
3.5kg(without magazine)
Magazine Capacity: 71-round drum
35-round box
Range: 200m(short bursts)
100m(long bursts)

This weapon was developed during World War 2 and is no longer in front line use with the Soviet Army although it is still used in many other parts of the world, especially the Middle and Far East.

It can be used either as a semi-automatic or as a full automatic and the change lever is on the trigger guard, forward for automatic and rearward for semi-automatic. It fires the M1930 'P' 7.62mm × 25 round, m/v being 500m/s, cyclic rate of fire is 700/900rpm but for practical purposes its rate of fire on semi-automatic is 40/50rpm and on full automatic 90/100rpm. Early weapons had the drum type magazine but later models

Below: *The 7.62mm Shapagin M1941 (PPSh) SMG.*

normally had the curved box magazine. The front sights are of the hooded post type with the rear-sights either tangent leaf (early models) or flip notch (later models).

The Shpagin M1941 ((PPSh) has also been built in many other countries including:

Communist China: Built as the Type 50 SMG, has box type magazine only, rear sight has apertures

Hungary: Built as the Type 48M, V-notch rear sight

Iran: Built both in 7.62mm and 9mm calibres, V-notch rear sight

North Korea: Built as the Type 49 with aperture rear sight

North Vietnam: Built as the Type K-50M, this is a Type 50 with a retractable metal stock

Yugoslavia: Built with many modifications as the M-49 or M-49/59

7.62mm Modernised Kalashnikov Assault Rifle (AKM) — Soviet Union

	AKM	AKMS
Calibre:	7.62mm	7.62mm
Length:	102cm	102cm(with bayonet)
	88cm	88cm(rifle only)
	——	64cm(stock folded)
Length of Barrel:	41.5cm	41.5cm
Weight:	3.6kg	3.8kg(loaded aluminium magazine)
	3.76kg	3.96kg(loaded late steel magazine)
	3.86kg	4.06kg(loaded early steel magazine)
	3.1kg	3.3kg(empty aluminium magazine)
	3.26kg	3.46kg(empty late steel magazine)
	3.36kg	3.56kg(with empty early steel magazine)
	2.93kg	3.13kg(without magazine)
Magazine Capacity:	30 rounds	30 rounds
Range:	400m	400m(semi-automatic)
	300m	300m(full-automatic)
Rate of Fire:	600rpm	600rpm(cyclic)
	100rpm	100rpm(full auto-practical)
	40rpm	40rpm(semi-auto practical)

The AKM is a development of the AK-47 Assault Rifle and the most significant difference is in the construction of the receiver. The AK-47 has a forged and machined receiver whilst the AKM has a stamped receiver. Mechanically the weapons are very similar but the AKM has a cyclic rate reducer in its trigger mechanism. As with the AK-47, there are two models of the AKM. The basic model which has a wooden stock is known as the AKM whilst that with a folding stock is known as the AKMS. Recognition features include radial gas ports on the gas cylinder, grasping rails on the handguard and the bayonet-lug. The foresight is of the pillar type with the rearsight of the U-notch type and graduated from 200 to 1 000m (the AK-47 is graduated to 800m). It can also be fitted with the NSP-2 infra-red night sight. The AKM fires the same 7.62 × 39mm cartridge with a m/v of 717m/s. The weapon has the same accessories as the AK-47 but its bayonet is of a different design and can also be used as a wire-cutter.

The AKM has also been built in a number of other countries including besides Poland:

East Germany One is a standard model with a conventional stock but with plastic grips and plastic handguard. The second model has a plastic stock, plastic grips and plastic handguard. They also have cleaning rods. In addition there is a training model which fires a .22 cartridge and is known as the KKMPi-1.

Hungary Hungarian-built AKMs have a perforated sheet metal forearm with a nylon foregrip. An SMG model has also been built with a muzzle-brake, rearsight graduated to 800m only and a folding stock.

Romania AKMs have a wooden pistol grip integral with the forestock.

The AKM entered service is 1959 and is both lighter than the AK-47 and easier to manufacture. More recently plastic and aluminium have been introduced into the weapon.

Top right: *The 7.62mm AKM Assault Rifle with a wooden stock.*
Above right: *The 7.62mm AKMS Assault Rifle with a folding stock.*

7.62mm Kalashnikov Assault Rifle (AK-47) Soviet Union

	Early Model	Late Model
Calibre:	7.62mm	7.62mm
Length:	107cm	107cm(with bayonet)
	87cm	87cm(stock extended)
	64.5cm	64.5cm(stock folded)
Length of Barrel:	41.5cm	41.5cm
Weight:	4.53kg	4.14kg(with loaded aluminium magazine)
	4.69kg	4.3kg(with loaded late steel magazine)
	4.79kg	4.4kg(with loaded early steel magazine)
	4.04kg	3.64kg(with empty aluminium magazine)
	4.2kg	3.8kg(with empty late steel magazine)
	4.3kg	3.9kg(with empty early steel magazine)
	3.87kg	3.47kg(without magazine)
Magzine Capacity:	30 rounds	30 rounds
Range:	400m	400m(semi-automatic)
	300m	300m(full-automatic)
Rate of Fire:	600rpm	600rpm(cyclic)
	100rpm	100rpm(automatic practical)
	40rpm	40rpm(semi-automatic)

The AK-47 was designed shortly after the end of World War 2 by Mikhail Kalashnikov and entered service with the Russian Army in 1951. It is no longer in front line service with the Warsaw Pact Forces having been replaced by the AKM which was developed from the AK-47.

The AK-47 has been built with both a wooden stock and a folding metal stock and there are also differences between early and late production models. Early models had a built-up receiver while late models had a straight rear ends to their receivers.

The AK-47 is gas-operated and fires a 7.62 × 39mm cartridge with a m/v of 717m/s. It is capable of full or semi-automatic fire, the selector is on the RHS of the receiver (up for safe, centre for

automatic and down for semi-automatic). Its sights are graduated to 800m. The foresight is of the pillar type and the rearsight is of the U-notch type.

The accessories for the AK-47 comprise a combination tool kit, a bayonet (two types — not interchangeable with those of the AKM, sling, blank firing device, night operations equipment (NSP-2 infra-red sight and a luminous sight), and a magazine carrier. There are four types of magazine for this weapon, two steel, one aluminium and one plastic.

The AK-47 has been manufactured in a number of countries including:

Bulgaria:

Communist China: Known as the Type 56 Assault Rifle and similar to the later production Russian models; recent models have a folding spike type bayonet. Type 56–1 is similar to the Soviet folding stock model.

Czechoslovakia: Although similar in appearance the *Czech* Vzor 58 Assault Rifle is in fact a different weapon in design.

East Germany: Known as the MPiK and MPiKS (folding butt). These do not have cleaning rods under the barrel or a recess in the butt for cleaning tools.

Finland: see M60 and M62 Assault Rifles, Page 31.

Hungary:

North Korea: Known as the Type 58 Assault Rifle.

Poland: The basic AK-47 is known as the PMK. The PMK-DGN-60 is used for launching the following grenades — DGN-60 HEAT anti-tank grenade with a range of 100m and the F1/N60 Fragmentation grenade with a range of 100/240m; this weapon has a ten-round magazine.

Romania:

Yugoslavia: three models, see separate entry (page 135).

Top: *The Standard 7.62mm Kalashnikov AK-47 Assault Rifle with wooden stock.*
Above: *The 7.62mm AK-47 with a folding metal stock.*

7.62mm Dragunov (SVD) Snipers Rifle — Soviet Union

Calibre: 7.62mm
Length: 122.5cm
137cm(with bayonet)
Length of Barrel: 62cm
Weight: 4.78kg(with 'scope, loaded magazine and bayonet)
4.52kg(with 'scope and loaded magazine)
4.3kg(with 'scope and empty magazine)
3.72kg(without 'scope and with empty magazine)
3.51kg(without 'scope and magazine)
Magazine Capacity: 10 rounds
Range: 1 300m(with 'scope)
800m(without 'scope)

The 7.62mm Dragunov SVD snipers rifle has replaced the M1891/30 sniper's rifle in the Warsaw Pact Forces. The weapon is easily recognisable by its skeleton stock with its small cheekpad, curved magazine and its sporting type barrel with gas cylinder above the barrel. A flash-suppressor is fitted at the end of the barrel and a standard AKM bayonet can be fitted if required. It fires the 7.62mm × 54R round with a m/v of 830m/s and its maximum rate of fire is 30rpm. The Dragunov is a gas-operated semi-automatic weapon and is related to the AK-47 family of weapons. Its normal sights are graduated to 1 200m. The PSO-1 telescopic sight has a × 4 magnification and a 6° field of view. It also has an integral rangefinder, a battery-powered reticle illumination system and an infra-red reconnaissance aid. This weighs .58kg and is graduated to 1 300m.

7.62mm Simonov (SKS) Carbine — Soviet Union

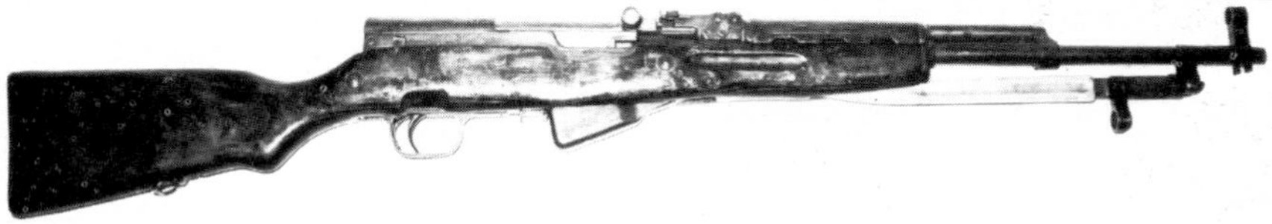

Calibre: 7.62mm
Length: 126cm(bayonet extended)
102cm(bayonet folded)
Length of Barrel: 52cm
Weight: 4.01kg(with loaded magazine)
3.85kg(with empty magazine)
Magazine Capacity: 10 rounds
Range: 400m(effective)

The Simonov carbine was designed by S. G. Simonov in 1944 and was standardised in 1945 as the 7.62mm semi-automatic carbine Simonov (SKS). It is no longer in front-line use with the Soviet Army having been replaced by the Kalashnikov assault-rifle. It is, however, still used for ceremonial purposes.

Early production models had a needle type folding bayonet but this was soon replaced by a knife type bayonet. The SKS is gas-operated and semi-automatic, it fires the 7.62mm × 39 cartridge, m/v being 735m/s. Normal rate of fire is 30rpm.

It is provided with a hooded front post and a rear tangent sight, and is sighted to 1 000m at 100m intervals. The SKS is easily recognisable by its bayonet, triangular integral magazine forward of the trigger and the gas port cylinder above the barrel. The Simonov has also been built in the following countries:

Communist China: known as the Type 56 with folding needle bayonet.
East Germany: known as the Karabiner S, also has a slot in the stock for carrying the weapon.
North Korea: built and known as the Type 63.
Yugoslavia: early models known as the M-59, later modified models were known as the M-59/66 (see separate entry).

As far as is known there are none of the following rifles left in service with the Soviet or any other army: Self-Loading 7.62mm Tokarev (SVT.38) Rifle, Self-Loading 7.62mm Tokarev (SVT 1940) Rifle, 7.62mm Tokarev Automatic Rifle (AVT 1940) and the 7.62mm Simonov Automatic Rifle (AVS.36).

Above: *The 7.62mm Simonov (SKS) Carbine.*

7.62mm Mossin Nagant M1944 Carbine — Soviet Union

Calibre: 7.62mm
Length: 133cm(with bayonet)
101.6cm(carbine only)
Length of Barrel: 51.8cm
Weight: 4.02kg(loaded with bayonet)
3,9kg(empty with bayonet)
Magazine Capacity: 5 rounds
Range: 400m

This is the carbine version of the M1891/30 rifle and is recognisable by its permanently attached needle bayonet which folds along the RHS when not in use. The earlier M1938 carbine is very similar but does not have a folding bayonet.

The M1944 fires the 7.62mm × 54R round, the m/v is 820m/s and average rate of fire is 10rpm. Its front sight is of the hooded post type and its rearsight is of the tangent notch type.

This weapon is no longer in front-line use with any of the Warsaw Pact Countries. It has been built in Communist China under the designation Type 53 Carbine. The Vietnamese used the Type 53 or the M1944 fitted with a spigot type grenade launcher known as the AT-44 rifle.

Below: *The 7.62mm Mossin Nagant M1944 Carbine.*

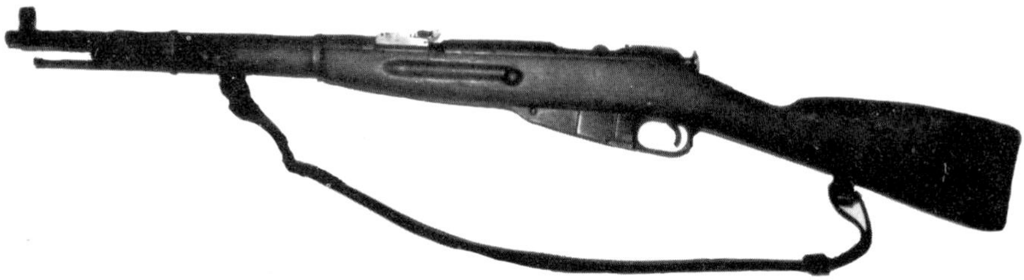

7.62mm Mossin Nagant M1891/30 Rifle — Soviet Union

Calibre: 7.62mm
Length: 123cm
Length of Barrel: .83m
Weight: 5.1kg(excluding sling)
Magazine Capacity: 5 rounds
Range: 800m(maximum effective)

This rifle entered service in 1930 and continued in production until 1944 and was one of the standard rifles of the Soviet Army during the World War 2. It was replaced by the M-1944.

The Mosin Nagant M1891/30 has a hooded post front sight, the rear sight is an adjustable tangent leaf sight with a V-notch. Usual rate of fire is 10rpm and it has a m/v of 862m/s. This weapon is also used as a sniper's rifle although this has been replaced in the Soviet Army by the new SVD rifle. The basic rifle has a straight bolt handle and the sniper's model has a longer turned-down handle. The sniper's model can be fitted with various types of telescope including the PE with a range of 1 400m and the PU with a range of 1 300m. The sniper's model does not have a bayonet. Both of these rifles fire the 7.62 × 54R rimmed round. The M1891/30 can be recognised by its sling holes in the stock, short straight bolt handle and its protruding magazine.

Other similar models to the M1891/30 rifle are the M1910 (no bayonet) and M1938 carbines and the M1891 (Dragon) rifle. The M1944 carbine is a shortened model of the M1891/30 and has a permanently attached folding needle type bayonet.

Top right: *The 7.62mm Mossin Nagant M1891/30 Rifle.*

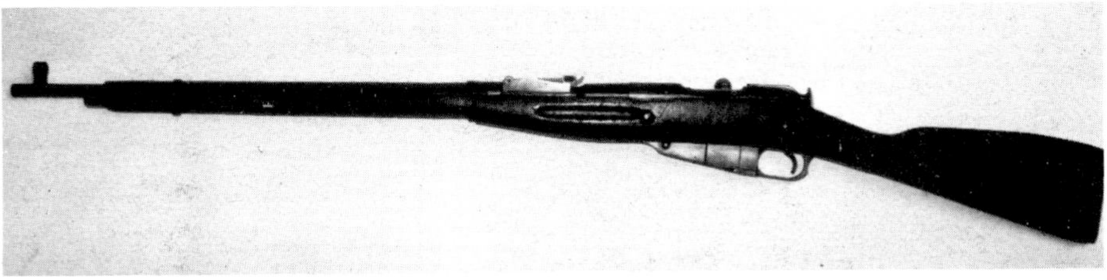

7.62mm Kalashnikov Light Machine Gun (RPK)

Soviet Union

Calibre: 7.62mm
Length: 103.5cm(overall)
82cm(RPKS with folded stock)
Length of Barrel: 59.1cm
Weight: 7.1kg(with loaded drum)
5.9kg(with loaded box)
5.9kg(with empty drum)
5.3kg(with empty box)
5kg(without magazine)
Magazine Capacity: 30-round AK-47/AKM box magazine
40-round RPK box magazine
75-round RPK drum magazine
Range: 800m
Rate of Fire: 600rpm(cyclic)
50/150rpm(practical)

The RPK is a gas-operated, selective-fire weapon that has been developed from the AK-47 Assault Rifle and is the replacement for the RPD Light Machine Gun.

The main differences between the AK-47 and the RPK are that the latter has a longer and heavier barrel, folding bipod, modified receiver, different rear sight and a different forearm and shoulder stock. The basic weapon is the RPK, the RPKS has a folding stock and this is normally issued to airborne troops.

The weapon fires the 7.62 × 39mm M1943 cartridge with a m/v of 732m/s and uses the same accessories as the AK-47 with the exception of the bayonet. Like the AK-47 the AKM can be fitted with an infra-red night sight. The RPK selector has three positions safe (top), full automatic (centre) and single shot (bottom). Its foresight is of the cylindrical post type and its rear sight is of the leaf notch type sighted from 100 to 1 000m.

Below: *The 7.62mm Kalashnikov Light Machine Gun (RPK).*

7.62mm Degtyarev (RPD) Light Machine Gun

Soviet Union

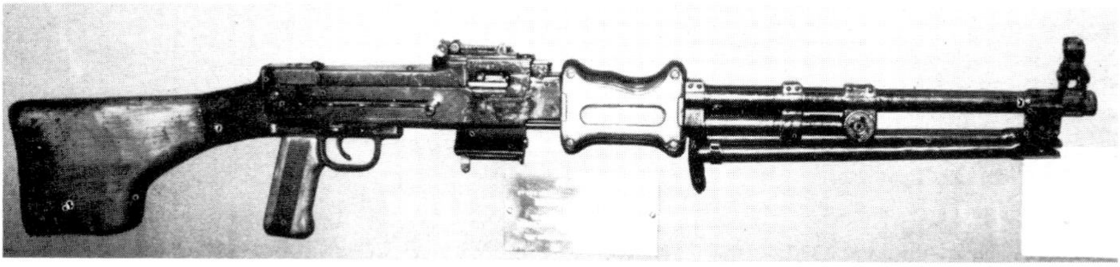

Calibre: 7.62mm
Length: 103.7cm
Length of Barrel: 52.3cm
Weight: 9kg(with loaded drum)
7.4kg(with empty drum)
6,6kg(without magazine)
Magazine Capacity: 100 rounds
Range: 800m
Rate of Fire: 650rpm(cyclic)
150rpm(practical)

The RPD (Ruchnoi Pulemet Degtyarev) entered production shortly after the end of World War 2 as a replacement for the DP and DPM LMGs. The RPD has itself now been replaced by the RPK LMG.

The RPD is recognisable by its short wooden stock, bipod, pistol-grip behind the trigger-guard and a wooden hand grip forward of the drum magazine. The RPD is a gas-operated full automatic weapon and fires the 7.62mm × 39 cartridge with a m/v of 753m/s. The drum holds two 50-round belts. The foresight is of the cylindrical post type and the rearsight is of the leaf tangent type sighted from 100 to 1 000m in increments of 100m. The NSP-2 night sighting devices can be used with this weapon.

There have been many models of the RPD LMG. These include the 1st model which had a cup type gas piston; the 2nd model which had a plunger type gas piston in place of the cup type and the windage knob was moved from the RS to the LS; the 3rd model was similar to the 2nd model but had dust covers on the feed mechanism and a folding non-reciprocating operating handle. This model was also built in Communist China as the Type 56; the 4th model is also known as the RPDM and is similar to the 3rd model but has a longer gas cylinder, an additional roller on the piston slide and a buffer in the butt; the 5th model was built only in Communist China where it was known as the Type 56-1, and is essentially a model RPDM with a magazine bracket/dust cover and a cleaning rod which is carried in the butt.

The RPD was built in a number of other countries including Hungary and North Korea, the Korean weapons being known as the Type 62.

Above: *The 7.62mm Degtyarev (RPD) Light Machine Gun.*

7.62mm Kalashnikov General Purpose Machine Gun (PK, PKS, PKT)

Soviet Union

Calibre: 7.62mm
Length: 117.3cm
Length of Barrel: 65.8cm(with flash suppressor)
Weight: 16.5kg(on tripod)
9kg(on bipod)
9.4kg(ammunition box and 250-round belt)
8kg(ammunition box and 200-round belt)
3.9kg(ammunition box and 100-round belt)
Range: 1 000m
Rate of Fire: 650rpm(cyclic)
250rpm(practical)

This is the current GPMG of most of the Warsaw Pact Forces and was designed by Kalashnikov who also designed the AK-47 Assault Rifle. The bolt mechanism is similar to that of the AK-47, the feed mechanism is similar to that of the Goryunov and Czech M59 weapons whilst the trigger mechanism is similar to that used on the Degtyarev MG.

When used with its bipod it is an LMG; ammunition is fed from a 100-round box magazine attached to the weapon. When used on a tripod (it still remains the bipod which folds up under the barrel when not required) it is fed from a 200 or 250-round box which is placed on the ground to the right of the weapon which weapon is then used as a heavy MG. When fitted in an AFV it is used as a co-axial weapon and operated by an electric trigger. It is then known as the PKT. The PKB is used externally on armoured vehicles.

A more recent model is the PKM—this is somewhat lighter than the earlier models. The barrel is unfluted and it also has a number of other modifications including a hinged butt rest. The PKMS is the PKM on a tripod.

The PK is belt-fed, air-cooled, and fully automatic. It fires the 7.62 × 54R cartridge with a m/v of 825m/s. Its gas regulator can be adjusted if required. The weapon is recognisable by its gas cylinder below the barrel, its frame type stock, carrying handle, pistol grip and folding bipod.

The barrel on the PK can be changed quickly. Early models had a cone shaped flash-hider but more recent models have a bar type supressor fitted similar to that on the American M60 MG. The PK has a cylindrical foresight and an adjustable rearsight. If required it can be fitted with an infra-red night fighting device.

It replaced the earlier RP-46 and SGM machine guns.

7.62mm RP-46 Machine Gun — Soviet Union

Calibre: 7.62mm
Length: 127cm
Barrel Length: 60cm
Weight: 15.8kg(with loaded drum)
14.57kg(with empty drum)
13kg(without drum or belt)
9.63kg(ammunition box and 250-round belt)
Magazine Capacity: 250-round belt
47-round drum
Range: 800-1 000m
Rate of Fire: 230/250rpm(practical)
600rpm(cyclic)
Crew: 2

The RP-46 MG is a post-war development of the DPM range. It is no longer in service with the Soviet forces but is still used by China, North Korea, North Vietnam and various 'Liberation Armies'. It has a carrying handle above the barrel rather like the British Bren LMG, a quick change barrel, bipod, pistol-grip, and an operating-spring housing which projects at the rear of the receiver. It fires the 7.62mm × 54R cartridge with a m/v of 840m/s. Although it can use a 47-round drum magazine (as used on the DP and DPM LMGs but without the belt feed mechanism), it normally uses a box with 250 rounds in 50-round metallic link belts. The PPN-2 night sighting device can be fitted to the RP-46. This weapon is also manufactured in Communist China as the Type 58 and in North Korea as the Type 64.

Below: *The 7.62mm RP-46 Machine Gun. (Type 58 shown.)*

7.62mm Goryunov M-1943 (SG-43) Machine Gun

Soviet Union

Calibre: 7.62mm
Length: 115cm
Barrel Length: 82.5cm(with flash hider)
72cm(without flash hider)
Weight: 36.9kg(gun and new wheeled mount)
40.4kg(gun and old wheeled mount)
27.4kg(gun and tripod)
13.5kg(gun only)
9.08kg(ammunition box and 250-round belt)
Magazine: 250-round fabric belt
50-round metallic belt
Range: 800/1 000m
500m anti-aircraft
Rate of Fire: 250/300rpm(practical)
500/700rpm(cyclic)
Crew: 2

The 7.62mm Goryunov MG entered service with the Russian Army during the World War 2 and is no longer in front line service with the Soviet forces. The first model to enter service was the SG; this had a smooth barrel, the sear attached to the driving-spring guide, a plain barrel lock, no dust covers and the operating handle between the spade grips. The second model was the SGM which has a splined barrel, a separate sear housing, a micrometer barrel lock and the operating handle on the right side of the weapon. The SGMT was a modified version for use on tanks and the SGMB was a modified version for use on armoured personnel carriers. The SG-43M is a reworked SG with the dust covers and barrel lock as with the SGMB. The last model is a GPMG type weapon developed by the Hungarians complete with pistol-grip trigger mechanism, butt stock and a bipod.

There are three types of mount for this weapon. The first M-1943 mount was on two wheels as was the latter Degtyarev mount. The more recent mount is the Sidorenko-Malinovsky tripod.

The weapon fires the 7.62mm × 54R round which has a m/v of 800m/s. Its front sight is of the blade type and its rearsight consists of a adjustable tangent leaf graduated from 200 to 2 300m in increments of 100m.

The SG is built in Communist China as the Type 53 whilst the SGMB is built there as the Type 57.

Below: *The 7.62mm Goryunov M-1943 (SG-43) Machine Gun. (SGM)*

7.62mm Degtyarev DP & DPM Light Machine Guns

Soviet Union

Calibre: 7.62mm
Length: 127cm
Length of Barrel: 60.9cm
Weight: 11.9kg(with loaded drum)
10.7kg(with empty drum)
9.1kg(without drum)
Magazine Capacity: 47-round drum
Range: 600m(practical)
Rate of Fire: 550rpm(cyclic)
80rpm(practical)

Note—data relates to DPM

The DP light machine gun was developed in the 1920's by Degtyarev and entered production in 1933. It was the standard LMG of the Soviet Army during the World War 2. The DP is gas-operated and full automatic firing the 7.62 × 54mmR round which has a m/v of 840m/s. The DA was an aircraft machine gun and the DT was a tank machine gun which had a folding stock and no barrel jacket.

The DPM, the M standing for modernised, was introduced in 1944. The modifications over the earlier DP included the fitting of a pistol-grip and a permanent bipod and the operating spring was removed from its position under the barrel, it is now longer and projects over the butt. The DPM has been built in Communist China as the Type 53 Light Machine Gun. The DPM was subsequently modified further to become the RP-46 (cf.). Neither of these weapons are now in front line Soviet use.

Below: *The 7.62mm Degtyarev DPM light Machine Gun.*

7.62mm Maxim M1910 (SPM) Machine Gun

Soviet Union

Calibre: 7.62mm
Length: 111cm
Barrel Length: 72cm
Weight: 69kg(gun, mount and shield)
46.38kg(gun, old type mount and no shield)
23.8kg(gun and coolant)
21.4kg(gun only)
9.08kg(ammunition box and a 250-round belt of ammunition)
Range: 1 000m(ground role)
500m(anti-aircraft role)
Rate of Fire: 250/300rpm(practical)
500/600rpm(cyclic)
Crew: 2–3

The Maxim M1910 MG was adopted by the Russian Army before the start of the World War 1 and continued in service with them until soon after the end of the World War 2. The first Maxims originated in England but in 1905 the Russians set up their own production line. The first model produced was the M1905 which had a bronze water-jacket, this was followed by the M1910 which had a plain steel water-jacket, the next model had a fluted casing and the final model (from 1942) had a large radiator type filler-cap on the top of the jacket. There were two mounts for the Maxim. The usual World War 2 mount was the so-called Sokolov mount which often had a shield, the second was the universal mount which could also be used in the anti-aircraft role.

The 7.62mm Maxim M1910 fires the 7.62mm × 54R cartridge, m/v 800m/s. Its front sight is of the protected blade type and the rear-sight is of the adjustable folding V-notch type.

The Maxim was phased out of the WPF many years ago but is still encountered in various parts of the world.

Above: *The 7.62mm Maxim M1910 (SPM) Machine Gun.*

12.7mm Degtyarev Shpagin M1938 and M1938/46 DShK Heavy Machine Guns

Soviet Union

Calibre: 12.7mm
Length: 158.8cm
Length of Barrel: 106.9m(with flash eliminator)
Weight: 131.5kg(gun and tripod)
34kg(gun only)
11kg(ammunition box and 50 rounds)
Magazine Capacity: 50-round belt
Range: 7 000m(maximum)
1 500m(effective range)
1 000m(anti-aircraft — effective range)
Rate of Fire: 540/600rpm(cyclic)
80/120rpm(practical)

The DShK entered service with the Soviet Army in 1938 and was a development of the earlier DK machine gun. The weapon is gas-operated and fully automatic, air-cooled and belt-fed. It fires the 12.7 × 108mm cartridge with a m/v of 860m/s which is fed in belts of 50. There is also an AP round which will penetrate 20mm of armour at 500m. The front sight is of the cylindrical post type and the rearsight is of the vertical leaf type which is graduated from 0–3 300m in increments of 100m. There is also a special A/A sight.

The DShK is now used in the Soviet Army as an tank machine gun (ie anti-aircraft with a reflex sight) or as a co-axial machine gun (ie on the T-10 tank). This is known as the DShKT. The DShK is still used in many countries in its original role as an HMG.

The M1938 has a revolving block type feed mechanism with an arched feed cover. The M1938/46 (which is also known as the DShKM) was developed after the World War 2 and has a belt-fed lever type feed mechanism and a rectangular cover. A flash eliminator was also introduced on this model.

The DShK can be used for both ground or anti-aircraft use. For the ground role the three legs are folded together to form the trail and the shield and wheels are retained. In the anti-aircraft role the wheels and the shield are removed and the trail legs form a tripod.

The M1938/46 is also built in China where it is known as the Type 54 HMG The Czechs have developed a 4-gun anti-aircraft model of this called the MG53 which is mounted on a chassis to give increased mobility.

The recognition features of the DShK are its flutted barrel, flash eliminators, its foresight about a quarter of the way down the barrel, its shield and its firing grips at the rear.

Top right: *The 7.62mm Degtyarev Shpagin M1938/46 DShK Heavy Machine Gun.*

Anti-Tank Grenade Launcher RPG-7V — Soviet Union

Calibre: 85mm(launcher)
40mm(tube)
Weight of Launcher: 6.3kg(including telescopic sight)
Length of Tube: 95cm
Range: 500m(stationary targets)
300m(moving targets)
Rate of Fire: 4–6rpm
Crew: 2

The RPG-7V is the standard rifle-squad anti-tank weapon of the Warsaw Pact Forces and is a recoilless, shoulder-fired, muzzle-loaded, reloadable weapon. It fires a PG-7V HEAT rocket, 925mm in length and weighing 2.2kg, with a muzzle velocity

Below: *The Anti-Tank Grenade Launcher RPG-7V.*

as it leaves the barrel of 100m/s. Within 10m a rocket motor fires and this boosts its velocity to 300m/s. The warhead weighs 1.75kg and will penetrate 320mm of armour. It has a piezo-electric fuze incorporating a self-destruct device which operates when the round is approx 900m from the launcher. There is also a training round called the PUS-7.

This weapon is recognisable by its two handgrips with the trigger on the foremost grip, optical sight on the LHS of the weapon and the funnel-shaped venturi at the rear.

The RPG-7V is fitted with a PGO-7 or PGO-7V optical sight which is marked from 200m to 500m at ranges of 100m. The sight has a 2½ × magnification and a 13° field of view. Open sights are provided for emergency use. If required this weapon can be fitted with the NSP-2 infra-red night sighting device.

The RPG-7D is a special model for the use of the airborne forces and can be quickly broken down into two components.

The RPG-7V is built in China under the designation of the Type 69 Anti-Tank Grenade Launcher.

82mm SPG-82 Anti-Tank Rocket Launcher

Soviet Union

Calibre: 82mm
Weight of Launcher: 37.85kg
Length of Tube: 206cm
Length Overall: 215cm
Range: 275m(stationary targets)
Crew: 2

The SPG-82 is also known as the SG-82 and is easily recognisable by its large shield, two-wheeled carriage and carrying handles. The weapon is no longer in use with any of the Warsaw Pact Forces but is still found in various parts of the world including the Middle East.

The SPG-82 can be fired from the prone position or from the shoulder, in the latter case it has to be supported by two men.

Without its fuze the HEAT projectile is 694mm in length and weighs 4.95kg. It has a muzzle velocity of 150m/s and will penetrate 120mm of armour. An HE round is also available for this weapon.

The weapon has two sets of sights. The inner set which is used for the HEAT projectile is marked for 100, 200 and 300m and the outer set, used for the HE round, is marked from 100 to 700m in 100m bands.

Anti-Tank Launcher RPG-2

Soviet Union

Calibre: 80mm(launcher)
40mm(tube)
Weight of Launcher: 2.86kg
Length of Tube: 95cm
Range: 150m(stationary targets)
75m(moving targets)
Rate of Fire: 4–6rpm
Crew: 1 or 2

The first Soviet anti-tank launcher was the RPG-1 which was a direct copy of the German Panzerfaust. The RPG-2 was a development of the German Panzerfaust 150 which was developed at the end of World War 2 but did not see service. The RPG-2 is no longer in service with the Soviet Army as it has been replaced by the more recent RPG-7V.

The RPG-2 is a muzzle-loaded, shoulder-fired, smooth-bore, recoilless weapon and is recognisable by its long tube and its grip with a built-in firing trigger. It cannot be fired from the left shoulder as there is a gas escape hole on the RHS near the firing mechanism.

The RPG-2 is also built in Communist China as the Type 56 Anti-Tank Grenade Launcher and was designated B-40 by the North Vietnamese and Viet Cong. Its open sights are graduated for 50, 100 and 150m. The weapon fires a PG-2 fin-stabilised HEAT grenade with a DK-4 base-detonating fuze and a self-destruct mechanism. Earlier grenades had the DK-2 fuze which did not have the self-destruct feature. The PG-2 weighs 1.84kg and is 500mm in length, muzzle velocity is 84m/s and it will penetrate 180mm of armour.

If required the RPG-2 can be fitted with the NSP-2 infra-red night sight. Some models have been fitted with a modified blast deflector at the rear.

Below: *The Anti-Tank Launcher RPG-2.*

50mm Mortar Model M40

Soviet Union

Calibre: 50mm
Weight: 11.5kg
Length of Barrel: 78.8cm
Elevation: + 45° and + 75°
Traverse(Total): 5½°
Range: 807m at 45° elevation
129m at 75° elevation
Crew: 2–3

Before World War 2, the Russians developed a series of lightweight 50mm mortars, these being designated the M38, M39, M40 and finally the M41. None of these are used by any of the Warsaw Pact Forces, but they are still used in some smaller countries and by some liberation forces.

The M40 was developed from the earlier M38 and it retained the earlier mortar's method of range adjustment. This is achieved by rotating a sleeve in the base of the mortar, this opened or closed a number of gas ports. To extend the range of the mortar the ports were all opened and to achieve the minimum range all of the ports were closed. The only type of mortar bomb available is a HE one with just one charge.

Right: *The 50mm Model M40 lightweight mortar.*

9mm Super Star Pistol

Spain

Calibre: 9mm
Length: 20.4cm
Length of Barrel: 13.3cm
Weight: 1.02kg
Magazine Capacity: 9 rounds
Muzzle Velocity: 366m/s
Maximum Effective Range: 50m

Over the years the Spanish armament industry has produced a bewildering array of pistols in a very wide range of calibres and designs, many of them cheap copies of existing pistols. Among the better of the Spanish pistols have been the products of the firm of Star Bonifacio Echeverria SA Eibar, and one of their products, the 9mm Super Star, is the current Spanish Army pistol. It combines some of the better design features of current American pistols and is a strong well-made weapon. Commercial versions have been sold in various calibres and are used by some police forces in several states.

9mm Star Model Z62 and Z-70/B Sub-Machine Guns

Spain

Calibre: 9mm
Length—Stock Folded: 48cm
Length of Barrel: 20.1cm
Weight Loaded: 3.55kg
Magazine Capacity: 30 rounds
Muzzle Velocity: 381m/s
Maximum Effective Range: 200m
Rate of Fire: 550rpm(cyclic)

The Z62 is gradually replacing the earlier Z45 in service with the Spanish Army. It has several novel features including an involved safety mechanism that prevents firing if the weapon is dropped, and a 'half-moon' trigger that gives single shots when the lower part of the trigger is pulled and automatic when pressure is applied to the top half. In service this latter feature has proved troublesome and the later Model Z-70/B has had the mechanism replaced by a conventional trigger—the later model is identical to the earlier version in all other respects. In use, the Star sub-machine guns have proved to be rugged and reliable weapons under a wide range of conditions.

9mm Star Model Z45 Sub-Machine Gun — Spain

Calibre: 9mm
Length—Stock Folded: 57.9cm
Length of Barrel: 19.8cm
Weight Loaded: 4.54kg
Magazine Capacity: 30 rounds
Muzzle Velocity: 381m/s
Maximum Effective Range: 200m
Rate of Fire: 450rpm(cyclic)

The Star Model Z45 was a Spanish design based on that of the German MP40 and was originally produced to a wartime German order. Production did not begin until mid-1944 and the weapon was issued to the Spanish Air Force and Civil Guard before being taken into service by the Spanish Army in 1949. The design differs from the MP40 in several respects, one of which is the barrel jacket, and the barrel which can be unscrewed from the front. Small numbers of this weapon were sold to Portugal, Cuba, Chile and Saudi Arabia. It is reported that some have been built in Indonesia.

7.62mm CETME Model 58 Rifle — Spain

Calibre: 7.62mm
Length: 101.6cm
Length of Barrel: 44.5cm
Weight—Metal Handguard and Bipod: 4.5kg
Weight—Wooden Handguard: 4.2kg
Magazine Capacity: 20 rounds
Muzzle Velocity: 762m/s
Maximum Effective Range: 600m
Rate of Fire: 550–650rpm(cyclic)
120rpm(automatic)
40rpm(single shot)

The CETME Model 58 has its origins in design work carried out in Germany during the World War 2. After May 1945 some research work continued in France but eventually a German design team moved to Spain where a 7.92mm CETME rifle was produced. Subsequent models were made in 7.62mm calibre and this version was selected for manufacture by Heckler and Koch as their G3 (qv). In 1958 the CETME (Centro de Estudios Tecnicos de Materiales Especiales) was selected for use by the Spanish Army as the Fusil d'Assalto CETME modelo 58. There are two versions which differ only in having wood or metal handguards, and there have been several production changes—the latest version is the Model C. The round used is different from the NATO 7.62mm round—it is a 7.62mm × 51 cartridge with a lighter bullet and less powerful charge. Optional extras are a bayonet, bipod, telescopic sight, infra-red night sight, and a special 5-round magazine for ceremonial or guard duties. Standard rifle grenades can be fired. The Model S is a sporting model.

CETME have also developed to prototype stage a 5.56mm assault rifle known as the Model L. This weighs 3.3kg and is 92cm in length, has a cyclic rate of fire of 750–800rpm, and muzzle velocity is 920m/s. Both fixed and retractable stock models have been built.

Above: *The 7.62mm CETME Model 58 Rifle.*

3.5 Inch Rocket Launcher Model 1965 — Spain

Calibre: 3.5in(88.9mm)
Length: 160cm(operational)
83cm(folded)
Weight: 5.4kg
Range: 450m
Crew: 1–2

This weapon is a further development of the Model 1953 and 1958 launchers which were based on the American M20 rocket launcher. The Model 1965 is built in Spain by Instalaza S.A. of Zaragoza, and is in service with the Spanish Army.

The firing mechanism is electric and the circuit is completed when a rocket is inserted into the barrel. The aiming mechanism consists of an elevating device and an optical sight. A regulator with two scales is positioned on the elevating device, one for anti-tank rounds with settings to 2 500m and the other for HE and smoke rounds with settings to 1 500m. The optical sight has a reticle engraved with elevation to 650m range. There are three types of rocket available for the Model 1965 and all are fin stabilised; they are issued in watertight plastic containers which float. The American M20-series launchers can be modified to fire these rockets.

HEAT Rocket CH M65
Weight: 2kg
Muzzle Velocity: 230m/s
Maximum range: 2 500m
Armour penetration: 330mm
Concrete penetration: 800mm

HE Rocket MB 66
Weight: 3.1kg
Muzzle velocity: 155m/s
Maximum range: 1 500m
Armour penetration: 250mm
Concrete penetration: 700mm

Incendiary Smoke FI M66
Weight: 2.7kg
Muzzle velocity: 155m/s
Maximum range: 1 500m

ECIA 60mm Commando Mortar — Spain

Calibre: 60.7mm
Weight: 5.9kg
3.1kg(barrel and breech)
2.8kg(baseplate)
Length of Barrel: 65cm
Range: 1070m
Rate of Fire: 30rpm(maximum)
Crew: 2 (1 man can carry the mortar complete)

This light mortar basically consists of a barrel and a very small base plate. The weapon can be held by one hand (the left) and the mortar bomb dropped in with the other. There is a canvas sleeve around the middle of the mortar's barrel to protect the hand from heat. A simple sight is provided. Ammunition used is the same as that used for the ECIA 60mm Mortar Model L.

Below: *The ECIA 60mm Commando Mortar in the firing position.*

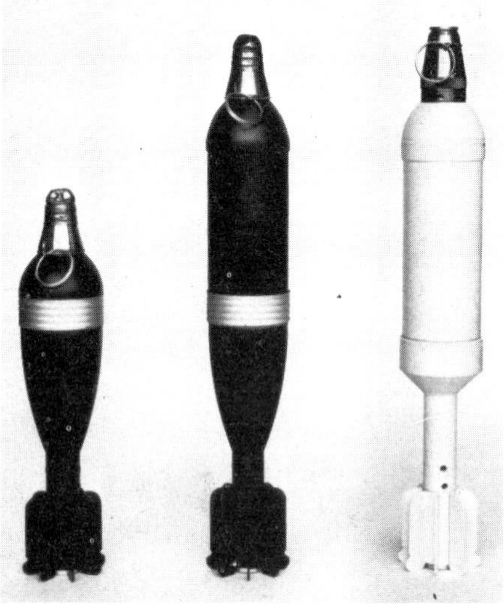

Left: *Mortar bombs for both the 60mm Model L and the 60mm Commando mortars. From left to right they are—High Explosive, High Capacity and Illuminating bombs.*

ECIA 60mm Mortar Model L

Spain

Calibre: 60.7mm
Total Weight: 12kg
4.2kg(barrel and breech piece)
2.8kg(baseplate)
3.9kg(mount)
1.1kg(sight)
Length of Barrel: 65cm
Range: 1 975m
Rate of Fire: 30rpm
Crew: 2 (1 man can carry the complete mortar)

This mortar is manufactured by Esperanza Y Cia. S.A. of Spain and is in service with the Spanish Army.

The mortar consists of a steel barrel, breech piece with a trigger mechanism, base plate, sight and tripod. The two unusual features of this mortar are its tripod (most mortars have a bipod) and its trigger which allows it to be fired either in the normal way (ie by gravity) or by trigger action.

The following types of ammunition have been developed for both the 60mm mortar Model L and the 60mm Commando mortar—HE and High Capacity HE Bombs and illuminating, smoke and practice bombs. There are a total of five charges. The HE Bomb is 263mm in length and weighs 1.43kg, it has a filling of .232kg of TNT and its maximum effective radius is 50m.

Left: *The ECIA 60mm Mortar Model L in the firing position.*

9mm Kulspruta Sub-Machine Gun m/45 — Sweden

Calibre: 9mm
Length—Stock Extended: 80.8cm
Length—Stock Folded: 55.2cm
Length of Barrel: 26.2cm
Weight Loaded: 5kg
Magazine Capacity: 36 rounds
Muzzle Velocity: 365m/s
Maximum Effective Range: 200m
Rate of Fire: 550–600rpm(cyclic)

Usually known as the 'Carl Gustav' and not to be confused with the rocket launcher of the same name (qv), the m/45 was first produced in 1945 and is still in production. It is the standard Swedish submachine gun and has been sold widely—Indonesia and Eire have been customers and the model was produced for a while in Egypt as the 'Port Said'. One version is the m/45B which can take a special 36-round wedge-shaped box magazine as well as the original 50-round box magazine adopted from the Finnish Suomi m/37-39, but the later models will accept only the 36-round magazine. The m/45 fires a special 9mm round with a thick jacket to increase penetration.

A silenced version of the m/45 was produced and used by American Special Forces in South-East Asia.

The Swedish firm of Husqvarna carried out some further development to the basic m/45 which resulted in the Hovea M49. This sub-machine gun is still used by the Danish Army, and is essentially similar in most respects to the m/45.

Below: *The 9mm m/45 Carl Gustav Sub-Machine Gun.*

5.56mm MKS Assault Rifle — Sweden

	MKS RIFLE	MKS CARBINE
Calibre:	5.56mm	5.56mm
Length Overall:	86.8cm	75.1cm
Length Stock Folded:	63.4cm	51.7cm
Length of Barrel:	46.7cm	35cm
Weight with Magazine and Sling:	3.36kg	2.97kg
Weight without Magazine:	2.75kg	2.36kg
Magazine Capacity:	30	30
Range:	400m	400m
Muzzle Velocity:	975m/s	925m/s
Rate of Fire:	700rpm(cyclic)	700rpm(cyclic)

The MKS has been developed by a new Swedish Company called Interdynamic AB of Stockholm. It has been designed specifically for export as the Swedish Army does not intend to adopt the small 5.56mm round at the present time. It has been designed for easy manufacture and extensive use is made of sheet metal components and moulded plastic.

The MKS uses the standard 5.56mm cartridge and fires from the closed bolt; it is gas-operated. The magazine is housed in the pistol grip and the stock can be folded through 180° so that it lays alongside the weapon. The barrel is provided with a combined flash-eliminator and grenade launcher; a bayonet can be fitted if required.

Either single shots or bursts can be selected. The foresight is of the hooded post type and the rearsight can be adjusted for both 250 and 400m ranges.

Top: *The 5.56mm MKS Rifle.*
Above: *The 5.56mm MKS Carbine.*

6.5mm Ljungman Rifles — Sweden

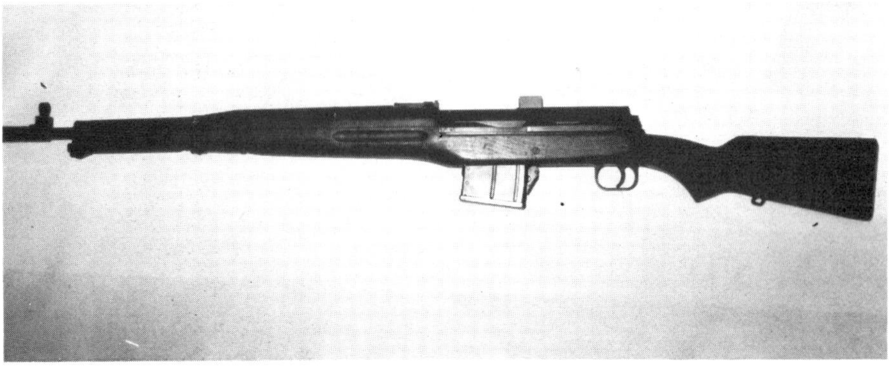

Calibre: 6.5mm
Length: 21.4cm
Length of Barrel: 62.2cm
Weight Empty: 4.71kg
Magazine Capacity: 10 rounds
Muzzle Velocity: 750m/s
Maximum Effective Range: 600m
Rate of Fire: 60rpm(single shot)

The first of the Ljungman semi-automatic rifles was designed in 1942 and entered service with the Swedish Army in late 1942 as the *halvautomatiskt gevar 42*. It was the first automatic rifle to see large scale service with any army and embodied a number of design features that have since been incorporated in such models as the Armalite AR-10 and AR-15. In 1953 some changes were made to produce the *halvautomatisck gevar* 42B (AG 42B). Both versions were produced by the Danish Madsen concern and a 7.92mm version was produced in Egypt as the 'Hakim' rifle. The AG 42B has now passed from first-line Swedish service and is used only by second-line and reserve units. It has been replaced by a locally-produced version of the Heckler and Koch G3, the AK-4.

Bottom left: *The 6.5mm Ljungman Rifle.*

Carl-Gustaf M2 84mm Rocket Launcher — Sweden

Calibre: 84mm
Weight of Gun: 14.2kg
Weight of Mount: .8kg
Weight of Telescopic Sight: 1kg
Weight of packed gun with accessories: 29.5kg
Length: 113cm

Range: 400m(HEAT round moving target)
500m(HEAT round stationary target)
1 000m(HE round)
1 000m(Smoke round)
2 000m(Illuminating round)
Rate of Fire: 6rpm
Crew: 2

The Carl-Gustaf is manufactured by FFV of Sweden and has been adopted by many countries. Although primarily an anti-tank-weapon various other types of ammunition have been developed which make the Carl-Gustaf a very useful infantry support

Below: *The Carl-Gustaf M2-550 84mm Rocket Launcher complete with sights and the FFV 551 HEAT round.*

IRO 84mm TPT 65
LOT Z73020

weapon. The normal crew is two men, one carries the launcher, and the other carries 8 rounds of ammunition.

The Carl-Gustaf is breech-loaded and percussion-fired. The round is fired by a side primer and the venturi is opened and closed with a rotary movement. The venturi must be in the closed position and locked by the fastening strap before the launcher can be fired.

The telescopic sight is mounted on the LHS of the weapon and has a $\times 2$ magnification and a 17° field of view. Luminous fore and rearsight adapters are available for use during night firing.

The following types of ammunition are available for the Carl-Gustaf:

FFV 65 HEAT Round: This weighs 2.6kg and will penetrate 400mm of armour, time of flight to 300m = 1.2 seconds; it has an electric fuze.

FFV 441 HE Round: Weight 3.1kg, time of flight to 700m = 3.4 seconds, can be fitted with an impact or air-burst fuze.

FFV 469 Smoke Round: Impact fuze and an instant smoke screen, weight 3.1kg.

Left: *The Carl-Gustaf M2 84mm Rocket Launcher in action.*

FFV 545 Illuminating Round: Weight 3.1kg, has a burning time of 30 seconds and will illuminate an area of 400–500m in diameter, 650 000 candelas.

For training there is an inert-filled Target Practice Tracer Projectile (TPT) which is the counterpart of the HEAT round. There is also a 6.5mm sub-calibre adapter for practice training.

Anti-Tank System FFV 550 (84mm Carl-Gustaf M2-550)

The FFV 550 is basically the standard M2 fitted with the new FFV 555 Sight and fires the new FFV 551 round. The FFV 555 Sight is an optical-electronic sighting system by means of which range and lead can be determined. This comprises a telescope, range-finder and a lead-finder. The sight has a maximum range of 1 000m and weighs 3.4kg; it has a $\times 3$ magnification and a 12° field of view.

FFV 551 HEAT Round: This round has been developed for use with the above sight. The complete round weighs 3kg with the projectile weighing 2.2kg. Maximum range is at least 700m which is achieved by a rocket motor starting after the shell has left the barrel. Muzzle velocity is 290m/s and maximum velocity is 380m/s. Time of flight to 400m is 1.2 seconds and to 700m, 2.1 seconds. This round will penetrate 700mm of armour. There is also a 7.62mm sub-calibre adapter for use with the FFV 550 System.

Miniman 74mm Anti-Tank Launcher — Sweden

Below: *The Miniman ready for action.*

Calibre: 74mm
Total Weight: 2.9kg
Total Length: 90cm
Range: 150m(moving targets)
250m(stationary targets)
Crew: 1 or 2

The Miniman is a lightweight recoilless weapon that can be used against both tanks and fortifications. The weapon is pre-loaded and instantly prepared for firing by removing the muzzle cover, erecting the sights and cocking the mechanical firing mechanism. Once the weapon is fired the Miniman is discarded. The HEAT shell weighs .88kg, has a muzzle velocity of 160m/second and will penetrate 340mm of armour. The shell is not armed until it is approx 10m from the muzzle of the weapon and is stabilised in flight by fins.

The barrel is made of glass-fibre reinforced plastic, the sights and firing mechanism are also of plastic and are bonded to the barrel. The combustion chamber is of high-strength aluminium alloy. The Miniman is waterproof and is normally carried by a sling.

A waterproof package is also available which carries two Miniman weapons, this is made of polystyrene with a covering of aluminium and will float if dropped in water. A 9mm sub-Calibre training device has been developed for the Miniman.

SIG Pistols

Switzerland

Calibre: 9mm
Length: 21.6cm
Length of Barrel: 12cm
Weight Empty: .909kg
Magazine Capacity: 8 rounds
Muzzle Velocity: 335m/s
Range: 50m

Data above relates to SIG P-210

The P-210 is manufactured by SIG in four basic models:
P-210-1: 120mm barrel for military and police duties, 9mm or 7.65mm calibre
P-210-2: 120mm barrel for military and police duties, 9mm or 7.65mm calibre
P-210-5: 150mm barrel for target shooting
P-210-6: 120mm barrel for target shooting.

If required the P-210-1/2 can be converted to .22 calibre. The system of operation is of the short recoil type. The difference between the P-210-1 and P-210-2 is that the P-210-1 has a polished finish whilst the P-210-2 has a sandblasted finish and is provided with a lanyard loop. Its foresight is of the blade type and its rearsight is of the notch type. The P-210-2 is used by a number of armed forces including Switzerland and Denmark.

Recently SIG have entered into an agreement with JP Sauer and the following pistols have recently entered production:
P220 which is available in .45, .38 and 9mm and can be converted to .22 calibre
P230 which is available in 9mm or 7.65mr models and can also be converted to .22 calibr with a simple kit.

Above: *The SIG 210-2 Pistol.*
Top right: *The P220 Pistol.*
Bottom right: *The P230 Pistol.*

SIG SAUER

SIG SAUER
9 mm Police

SIG 540 and SIG 542 Automatic Rifles — Switzerland

	SG 540	SG 542
Calibre:	5.56mm	7.62mm
Length Overall:	95cm	100.2cm
Length with Butt Folded:	71.4cm	74.8cm
Length of Barrel:	49cm	49.5cm
Weight with Fixed Butt and W/O Bipod and Mag:	3.12kg	3.36kg
Weight with Bipod:	3.54kg	3.86kg
Magazine Capacity:	20 rounds	20 or 30 rounds
Range:	400m	400m
Rate of Fire:	650/800rpm	650/800rpm(cyclic)
	90rpm	80rpm(automatic)
	40rpm	40rpm(single shots)

Some years ago SIG developed a weapon called the SG 530-1 in 5.56mm calibre, both long and short barrelled models were built as were both fixed and folding-stock models, none of these, however, went into production.

The SIG 540 fires the 5.56mm × 45 cartridge with a m/v of 980m/s whilst the SG 542 fires the 7.62mm × 51 cartridge with a m/v of 820m/s. At the present time the SG 540 is not in production although some orders have been received for the SG 542.

The weapons are gas-operated with a rotating bolt. The foresight is of the cylindrical post type whilst the rearsight is of the aperture type. The SG 540 is graduated from 100 to 500m and the SG 542 from 100 to 600m. It is available with a fixed stock or a folding butt; a bipod can be provided. Optional equipment includes a bayonet, telescopic sight, night sight and a three-round burst control device.

Below: *The SIG 542 Automatic Rifle.*

SIG 510-4 7.62mm Automatic Rifle — Switzerland

Calibre: 7.62mm
Length: 101.5cm
Length of Barrel: 50.5cm
Weight: 4.25kg(gun only)
4.56kg(with bipod)
Magazine Capacity: 20 rounds
Range: 600m
Rate of Fire: 60rpm(cyclic)
80rpm(automatic)
40rpm(single shots)

The standard rifle of the Swiss Army is the SIG built AM55 (StGW57). The SIG 510 series were developed from the earlier weapon and there are the following models in the range:

SIG 510-1 for 7.62mm × 51 NATO round
SIG 510-2 for 7.62mm × 51 NATO round (lighter model)
SIG 510-3 for the 7.62mm × 39 Soviet round
SIG 510-4 for the 7.62mm × 51 NATO round; there is also a sporting model called the SG-AMT.

The SIG 510-4 is the only member of the family that has been sold in any great quantity and most of these have gone to South America. The weapon's system of operation is of the delayed blowback type with a semi-rigid breech. It has a selector for single shot or full automatic and a bipod is provided.

The rearsight is of the aperture type and the front sight is of the cylindrical post type; the rearsight is graduated from 100 to 600m in 100m increments. On the SIG 510-3 it is sighted to 500m only.

A wide range of accessories are available including a × 4 telescope, sling, bayonet and night sight. Anti-tank grenades can be fired from this weapon.

Bottom left: *The SIG 510-4 7.62mm Automatic Rifle complete with bipod.*

7.51mm M-31 (Schmidt-Rubin) Rifle 7.51mm M-31/55 Sniper's Rifle — Switzerland

	M-31	M-31/55
Calibre:	7.51mm	7.51mm
Length:	110.4cm	121cm
Length of Barrel:	65.2cm	65.5cm
Weight:	4.01kg	5.53kg
Magazine Capacity:	6	6
Muzzle Velocity:	780m/s	—
Range	400m	400/600m
Rate of Fire	12rpm	12rpm

In 1889, two men, Colonel Schmidt and Colonel Rubin, developed a rifle which became known as the Model 1889 and this was adopted by the Swiss Army. After this came the Model 1889/96, the Model M1897 which was a single-shot rifle for training purposes, the Model 89/00 was a shorter model for the use of fortress troops, the M1905 was a light carbine model whilst the Model 1896/11 was chambered for the M1911 cartridge. The next model was the M-31 (or K-31 = Karabiner 31).

Below: *The 7.51mm M-31 Schmidt-Rubin Rifle.*

The M1931/42 was a sniper's rifle with a telescope, magnification × 1.8, the M1031/48 was a sniper's rifle with a telescope, magnification × 2.8. The current sniper's rifle is known as the M1935/55 and is provided with a telescope, magnification of × 3.5, a muzzle brake, and a bipod.

7.51mm MG51 Machine Gun — Switzerland

Calibre: 7.51mm
Length: 127cm
Length of Barrel: 56.4cm
Weight: 15.8kg
27kg complete with tripod
Range: 1 000m with tripod
Rate of Fire: 1 000rpm

The MG51 (Maschinengewehr Model 1961) is the standard machine gun of the Swiss Army. The weapon can be used with either a bipod or a tripod. When being used with the latter the bipod is folded up underneath the barrel. Ammunition is in belts of 250.

The Swiss Army also used a light machine gun called the LMG 25 (Leichtes Maschinengewehr 25); this is fed from a 30-round magazine on the RHS. Its cyclic rate of fire is 450rpm, and its maximum effective range is 800m. The weapon is normally used with a bipod although a tripod is also available.

SIG 7.62mm 710-3 Machine Gun — Switzerland

Calibre: 7.62mm
Length: 114.6cm
Length of Barrel: 56cm
Weight: 9.65kg(gun)
.7kg(bipod)
2kg(standard barrel)
2.3kg(heavy barrel)
10.2kg(tripod)
Range: 2 200m(tripod)
800m(bipod)
Rate of Fire: 800/900rpm(cyclic)
200/300rpm(automatic)

The 7.62mm 710-3 machine gun was designed over ten years ago by SIG of Neuhausen Rhine Falls. To date, however, it has not been produced in large quantities. It can be used in both the LMG role with a bipod or in the heavy role with a tripod and a heavy barrel. It can be fitted with an ammunition box holding 100 rounds.

It fires a standard NATO cartridge with a m/v of 790m/s. System of operation is delayed blow-back with stationary barrel and semi-rigid roller type breech. Ammunition is fed from the left via steel belts or disintegrating belts.

The foresight is of the protected blade type and the rearsight is of leaf type graduated from 100

Below: *The SIG 7.62mm 710-3 Machine Gun on L 810 Tripod.*

to 1 200m in increments of 100m. Early models had a wooden butt, but more recent models have a metal stock.

A wide range of accessories are available including a × 2.5 telescopic sight, infra-red night sight, and a tripod mount.

83mm M58 Anti-Tank Weapon Switzerland

Calibre: 83mm
Weight: 7.5kg(unloaded)
Length: 130cm
Range: 200m(effective)
Crew: 1–2

This Swiss-designed weapon is known as the 8.3cm Raketenrohr 58 by the Swiss Army. It fires a round weighing 1.82kg with a muzzle velocity of 200m/s. It is provided with a shield which has a sighting window to protect the operator when the weapon is fired.

American Revolvers

Although there are now no revolvers still in use with the American forces, so many thousands have been produced over the years that it would be futile to suggest that any one of the numerous models produced is no longer in military service. By its very nature the revolver is sturdy and efficient and requires less maintenance than its automatic counterpart. As a result, in many places the revolver is still used by military police, rear-echelon and para-military forces. Space precludes a complete breakdown of all the American types still in use and mention of the American revolvers has been limited to a listing of the types most likely still to be encountered:

Smith and Wesson .38/200
Smith and Wesson Hand Ejector Revolver M1917
Smith and Wesson .38 Model No 10
Smith and Wesson .38 Model No 12
Smith and Wesson .38 Model No 15
Smith and Wesson .38 Models No 37 and 38 'Airweight'
Colt .45 New Service M1917
Colt .38 Agent
Colt .38 Police Special
Colt .38 or .357 Magnum Mark 111 Lawman

This list is by no means fully comprehensive but merely gives an idea of the types likely to be in service. Note that as a general rule the superpowerful Magnum rounds have yet to be fully accepted as service issue although they are widely used by law enforcement agencies and may therefore be used by military police units.

.45 M1911 and M1911A1 Automatic Pistol United States

Calibre: .45in(11.43mm)
Length: 21.91cm
Length of Barrel: 12.78cm
Weight Loaded: 1.36kg
Weight Empty: 1.13kg
Muzzle Velocity: 252m/s
Maximum Effective Range: 20m
Magazine Capacity: 7 rounds

The Colt M1911 was taken into US Army service in 1911 and ever since has remained in use with the American Army and a host of other armies throughout the world. It has also been licence-built and copied by a number of other countries (many Spanish pistols are based on the M1911). In 1926 some minor changes were introduced to produce the M1911A1 but these changes did not effect the status of the M1911 which remains in use. During World War 2, the M1911A1 was produced in thousands by a number of firms and was freely distributed to a number of countries. Today, the M1911A1 is still used by the US Army and by Taiwan, South Korea and the Phillipines. The bullet fired is a 230g projectile (.45 Ball 1911) and an unusual round is the .45 High Density Shot M261 which comprises 16 ball-shot projectiles enclosed in a ball round sabot for use against massed personnel at close range. The conventional ball round has prodigious man-stopping qualities but the heavy recoil make the pistol rather awkward to handle with accuracy and training is needed to use it effectively.

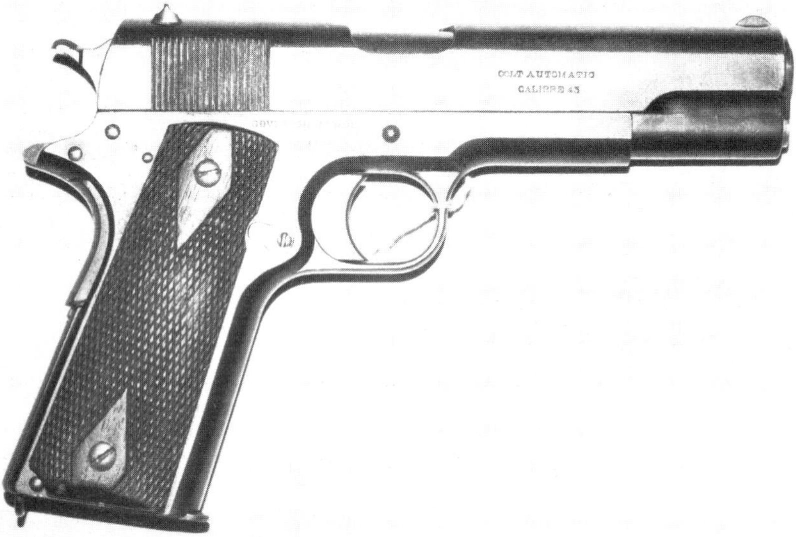

Above: *The .45 M1911A1 Automatic Pistol.*

Ingram M-10 Sub-Machine Guns — United States

Calibre: .45in(11.43mm) or 9mm
Length—Stock Extended: 54.8cm
Length—Stock Retracted: 26.9cm
Length—No Stock: 26.7cm
Length of Barrel: 14.6cm
Weight Loaded(30 rounds): 3.82kg
Weight Empty: 2.84kg
Magazine Capacity: 30 or 32 rounds
Muzzle Velocity—.45: 280m/s
Muzzle Velocity—9mm: 366m/s
Maximum Effective Range: 100m
Rate of Fire(.45): 1145rpm(cyclic)
90rpm(automatic)
40rpm(single shot)

Gordon B. Ingram has designed and produced a number of sub-machine guns since 1945. His Model 6 was produced for various American police forces, the Cuban Navy and for Peru, but subsequent models did not do so well until Ingram produced the Model 10 in 1970. The Model 10 has obvious affinities with the Uzi sub-machine gun but the construction methods are different and the M-10 is much smaller. Because of the light bolt, the rate of fire of the M-10 is high but it is intended for firing in short bursts only. Despite an energetic sales campaign the M-10 has been sold only to Chile and Yugoslavia although many countries have bought trial batches and many police forces now use some for law enforcement. The M-10 can be bought in .45in or 9mm calibre and a smaller lighter version, the M-11, is available in .380 calibre.

Bottom left: *The Ingram M-11 Sub-Machine Gun.*

.45 M3 and M3A1 Sub-Machine Guns United States

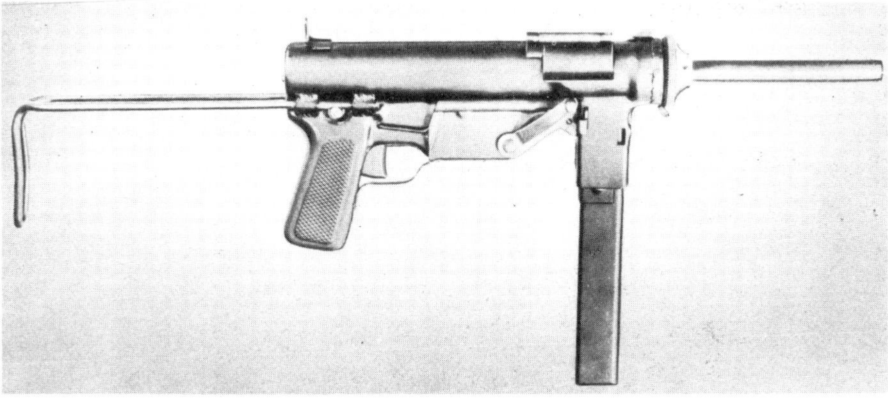

Calibre: .45in(11.43mm) and 9mm
Length—Stock Extended: 75.7cm
Length—Stock Retracted: 57.9cm
Length of Barrel: 20.3cm
Weight Loaded and Complete(M3A1): 4.52kg
Magazine Capacity: 30 rounds
Muzzle Velocity: 280m/s
Maximum Effective Range: 200m
Rate of Fire: 450rpm(cyclic)
120rpm(automatic)

When America entered the war in 1941 there was a shortage of sub-machine guns and the Thompson was proving difficult to mass-produce. The example of the British Sten and German MP40 was taken as the starting point of what became the M3 sub-machine gun, a simple all-metal weapon designed for easy and cheap production. The M3 was produced in very large numbers and was replaced in production by the M3A1 which was an even simpler design in which the cocking handle was replaced by a finger hole in the breech block. The M3A1 was kept in production until the Korean War and many were distributed to Taiwan and the Phillipines and many more were sold to South American countries. Many of the Far East examples are in 9mm calibre. The basic M3 design has been extensively copied 'unofficially'—typical examples are the Argentinian P.A.M. 1 and 2 in 9mm, and the Chinese Type 36 (.45) and 37 (9mm).

Above: *The .45 M3 Sub-Machine Gun which was also known as the 'grease gun'.*

The Thompson Sub-Machine Guns

United States

M1928A1
Calibre: 0.45in(11.43mm)
Length Overall: 85.2cm
Length Minus Butt: 63.5cm
Weight Loaded(30 rounds): 5.63kg
Weight Empty: 4.9kg
Magazine Capacity: 20 or 30-round box, 50-round drum
Muzzle Velocity: 282m/s
Maximum Effective Range: 200m
Rate of Fire: 700rpm(cyclic)
120rpm(automatic)
40rpm(single shot)

The Thompson sub-machine gun was the first American sub-machine gun, and development started during World War 1. The first model was the Model 1921 but production and sales were slow despite a number of design changes and the impetus given by the 'gangster era'. The first true military model was the M1928A1 which was standardised in 1938, and war production produced the M1 and M1A1. These last two models were produced by the thousand despite the unsuitability of the Thompson for mass-production. In service the Thompson proved bulky and rather complex to maintain but it was used all over the world and gained a formidable reputation as a close-combat gun. After 1945 its cost and weight were the deciding factors in its being replaced by more modern weapons and today the Thompson has almost entirely vanished from the military scene. It remains in small-scale service in Egypt, Haiti and Yugoslavia, and many have found their way into the hands of the IRA. Numerous 'unofficial' copies have been made by some small countries, typical of which are the crude copies made in China and used in Vietnam.

Below: *The famous Thompson Sub-Machine Gun.*

5.56mm Ruger Mini-14 Rifle

United States

Calibre: 5.56mm
Length: 94.6cm
Length of Barrel: 47cm
Weight Empty: 2.9kg
Weight Loaded(20 rounds): 3.1kg
Magazine Capacity: 5, 20 or 30 rounds
Muzzle Velocity: 1 005m/s
Maximum Effective Range: 300m
Rate of Fire: 40rpm(semi-automatic)

With the Mini-14 rifle, Ruger have made a return to 'conventional' firearm construction while at the same time using the modern small-calibre 5.56mm round. The action is basically that of the M1 Garand rifle scaled down to suit the new cartridge. This action has been retained as it has proved strong and reliable over the years and the Mini-14 is designed for a long life and rugged treatment. The stock is made from hardwood in a style not seen in military firearms for some years and the metal used for the mechanism and receiver is high-grade steel. Ammunition can be either the 5.56mm × 45 cartridge or any commercial equivalent. As yet the Ruger Mini-14 has been purchased by few military buyers but its sound construction means it should be a very attractive proposition for many armies.

Top right: *The 5.56mm Ruger MINI-14 Rifle.*

5.56mm Armalite AR-18 — United States

Calibre: 5.56mm
Length—Stock Extended: 94cm
Length—Stock Folded: 73.6cm
Length of Barrel: 47.6cm
Weight Loaded: 3.58kg
Magazine Capacity: 20 rounds
Muzzle Velocity: 990m/s
Maximum Effective Range: 400m
Rate of Fire: 750–800rpm(cyclic)
80rpm(automatic)
40rpm(single shot)

The AR-18 is a development of the AR-15 which has been carried out by Armalite to produce a modern weapon which can be fabricated and assembled by relatively simple and cheap machinery. The AR-15 for all its advantages requires relatively complex and expensive production facilities, and in many parts of the world these are not available. The AR-18 therefore makes use of metal stampings, welding, and plastic where possible. Although not accepted for use by the US Army, the AR-18 has been extensively tested by them. Production is under way by Armalites at Costa Mesa in California, in Japan, and in the UK the Sterling Armament Company are preparing for production. As well as the basic AR-18, two other models are available— the AR-18S which is a shortened submachine gun version, and the AR-180 which can fire semi-automatic only and cannot be easily converted for full automatic fire.

Above centre: *The AR-18 complete with telescopic sight.*
Above: *The AR-18 with stock folded back.*

5.56mm Stoner 63 System

United States

Calibre: 5.56mm
Length: 102.2cm
Length of Barrel: 50.8cm
Weight: 4.39kg(with 30 rounds)
3.51kg(weapon only)
Range: 400m
Muzzle Velocity: 1 000m/s
Rate of Fire: 600rpm(cyclic)
90rpm(automatic)
40rpm(single shots)

The Stoner 63 system was designed by the Cadillac Gage Company, the first prototypes being completed in 1962. These were chambered for the standard 7.62mm × 51 NATO cartridge. There followed a model chambered for the 5.56mm × 45 cartridge and this round was subsequently adopted for the complete range of weapons.

The system itself is designed around the same receiver, bolt and piston, return spring, trigger and firing mechanism. From those components the following weapons could be built up—sub-machine gun, assault rifle, light machine gun (belt fed), light machine gun (magazine fed), medium machine gun and a machine gun suitable for installation in armoured vehicles.

The weapons are gas-operated and system of locking is of the rotating bolt type. The foresight is of the cylindrical post type and the rearsight is of the flip aperture type.

The LMG was used in Vietnam by the United States Marine Corps as the XM207. The other components of the system have not been produced in quantity although licences were issued to the Dutch company of NWM who no longer build weapons.

Below: *The Stoner 63 Assault Rifle.*

5.56mm Colt Commando

United States

Calibre: 5.56mm
Length — Butt Extended: 78.7cm
Length — Butt Retracted: 71.1cm
Length of Barrel: 25.4cm
Weight Loaded: 3.23kg
Magazine Capacity: 20 or 30 rounds
Muzzle Velocity: 924m/s
Maximum Effective Range: 200m
Rate of Fire: 700–800rpm(cyclic)
150–200rpm(automatic)
40–50rpm(single shot)

The Colt Commando is a shortened version of the M16 rifle (qv) developed for use in the jungles of SE Asia and in most details, apart from the length, is identical to the M16 in handling, appearance and mechanism. It has been used in action in Vietnam by special forces under the designation of XM177E2, but at present its future is uncertain. Accuracy and handling when fired tend to be impaired by the short barrel.

Bottom left: *The 5.56mm Colt Commando.*

5.56mm M16 and M16A1 Rifles — United States

Calibre: 5.56mm
Length with Flash Suppressor: 99cm
Length of Barrel: 50.8cm
Weight Empty(M16A1): 3.18kg
Weight Loaded(M16A1 with 30 rounds): 3.82kg
Magazine Capacity: 20 or 30 rounds
Muzzle Velocity: 990m/s
Maximum Effective Range: 400m
Rate of Fire: 700–950rpm(cyclic)
150–200rpm(automatic)
45–65rpm(semi-automatic)

The M16 rifle is the Armalite AR-15 designed by Eugene Stoner and is a logical development of the AR-10. Using the smaller 5.56mm × 45 cartridge, the AR-15 is a much smaller and lighter weapon than its predecessor and thus has definite handling, supply and 'handiness' advantages. The US Air Force was first to obtain the AR-15 as the M16 and the US Army then bought the type as the M16A1 which differs in having a bolt closure plunger on the RHS of the receiver. The M16A1 is now the standard rifle of the US Army and to date well over 3 000 000 have been produced. The M16A1 was introduced into service when the US Army was in action in Vietnam and many early troubles arose from inadequate training and changes in the ammunition specification. These troubles were, however, eradicated and the M16 series is now a reliable service weapon. It has been widely exported and is licence-built in Singapore, South Korea and the Philippines. The UK has bought a small batch for use in the Far East and by Ghurka units. Many Far East nations have bought the M16 as its light weight and small size make it ideal for handling by the small-statured races of that part of the world. Other user nations are Jordan, Taiwan and Italy (special service units only).

The M16 and M16A1 are manufactured by Colt Fire Arms Inc, although some have been made by

Below: *The 5.56mm M16A1 complete with bipod.*

Harrington and Richardson, and the Hydramatic Division of General Motors. The mechanism is gas-operated and fire can be full automatic or semi-automatic. A bipod can be fitted, as can a bayonet. The flash suppressor, which is fixed, can be used to fire standard rifle grenades. An extra attachment is the M203 40mm Grenade Launcher which fits below the barrel (replacing the earlier M79 Grenade Launcher). The M203 fires one shot at a time and has a maximum range of 350m, although its effective range is 150–200m. A wide variety of ammunition is available for the M203 including HE, fragmentation, armour piercing and illuminating.

Left: *The 5.56mm M16A1 being used by a British Gurkha soldier.*
Below: *The M203 40mm Grenade Launcher attachment mounted on standard M16A1 Rifle.*

7.62mm AR-10 Assault Rifle — United States

Calibre: 7.62mm
Length: 102.9cm
Length of Barrel: 50.8cm
Weight Empty: 4.24kg
Weight Loaded: 4.82kg
Magazine Capacity: 20 rounds
Muzzle Velocity: 845m/s
Maximum Effective Range: 500m
Rate of Fire: 700rpm(cyclic)
80rpm(automatic)
40rpm(single shot)

The Armalite AR-10 was produced originally as an assault rifle in .30 calibre but this was soon changed to accommodate the 7.62mm × 51 NATO cartridge. There were many design features built into the AR-10 that were later to be incorporated into the AR-15 but the AR-10 had little commercial success as it was brought out at the time of the move away from the 7.62mm calibre to the smaller 5.56mm. Plans to produce the weapon in Holland came to nothing and the only sales were of small batches to the Sudan, Burma, Portugal and Nicaragua. Trial models of the AR-10 were produced as light machine guns using either magazine or belt feeds. A carbine model was also made. None of these trial models were produced for sale, but many features were designed into later Armalite products.

Above: *The AR-10 7.62mm Assault Rifle.*

7.62mm M14A1 Rifle

United States

Calibre: 7.62mm
Length Overall: 112cm
Length of Barrel: 55.9cm
Weight Loaded: 6.6kg
Magazine Capacity: 20 rounds
Muzzle Velocity: 853m/s
Maximum Effective Range with Bipod: 700m
Maximum Effective Range W/O Bipod: 460m
Rate of Fire: 700–750rpm(cyclic)
60rpm(automatic)
40rpm(single shot)

The M1 Garand rifle served the American forces well but its weight and small magazine were held to be undesirable features by the early 1950's and much experimental work went on to produce a lighter, full automatic version. When the 7.62mm

Below: *The M14A1 7.62mm Rifle with bipod.*

× 51 NATO round was selected in 1953 a new rifle based on the Garand was adopted. This rifle had a long development history and was selected for production as the M14. This was basically a Garand mechanism updated to give automatic fire and in 1968 the M14A1 went into production with better facilities for full automatic fire, including a bipod. The M14 and M14A1 had a relatively short front-line service life despite the fact that about 1 500 000 were produced. It is now relegated to National Guard units, but one variant, the Rifle 7.62mm M21, is still in use as a specialist sniper rifle. The M21 is carefully assembled and fires only match ammunition. Many M-14 and M14A1 rifles are still in use around the world and the type has been licence-built in Taiwan. Nations using the M14 include South Korea and the type was also used by South Vietnam.

.30 M1 Carbine

United States

Calibre: .30in(7.62mm)
Length—M1: 90.4cm
Length—M1A1 Stock Extended: 90.5cm
Length—M1A1 Stock Folded: 64.8cm
Length of Barrel: 45.8cm
Weight Loaded—M1: 2.63kg
Weight Loaded—M1A1: 2.77kg
Weight Loaded—M2: 2.63kg
Magazine Capacity: 15 or 30 rounds
Muzzle Velocity: 607m/s
Maximum Effective Range: 300m
Rate of Fire—M2: 750rpm(cyclic)
75rpm(automatic)
40rpm(single shot)

The M1 Carbine was designed by Winchester in 1940 and 1941 in answer to a call for a light rifle to replace the pistol in rear echelon units and increase their potential fire power. It went into production in late 1941 and by the time production ceased well over 6 000 000 had been made. The basic M1 was a semi-automatic weapon and the M1A1 had a folding stock. A later version, the M2, was capable of automatic fire, and a further version, the M3 was a special 'sniper' variant. There were numerous other experimental versions but few went into service. The M1 and M2 were eventually issued to front-line combat units for use by officers and NCOs, but has now been largely replaced by the M-16 with the American forces except for some National Guard units. The M2 remains in service in Ethiopia, Chile, Taiwan, Honduras, Japan, Cambodia, South Korea, Laos, Mexico, Norway, the Philippines and Tunisia. The M1 and M2 have been produced under licence by Beretta for the Italian Army as the Model 1957 (also sold to Morocco), and have been copied in Dominica as the Cristobal Carbine M2.

Above: *The .30 Carbine M1.*

.30 Rifle M1 (Garand)

United States

Calibre: .30in(7.62mm)
Length: 110.7cm
Length of Barrel: 61cm
Weight Empty: 4.3kg
Magazine Capacity: 8 rounds
Muzzle Velocity: 865m/s
Maximum Effective Range: 600m

The M1 Rifle, often referred to as the Garand after its designer, was adopted as standard for the US forces in 1932. Production began in 1937 and did not end until the mid-1950's by which time about 5 500 000 had been made. The M1 was the first semi-automatic rifle to be selected for service and although numerous experimental versions were made the basic design remained unchanged throughout its service life. The rifle is loaded with an eight-round clip—single round loading is not possible—and the mechanism is gas-operated. Since 1945 the M1 has been issued or sold to many nations, and one, Italy, has produced the M1 under licence for the Italian Army as the Fucile

M-1 Garand (some of these have been re-chambered for the 7.62mm NATO round). Among user nations are Chile, Taiwan, Costa Rica, Denmark (m/50), Greece, Guatemala, Haiti, Indonesia, Iran, Japan, Jordan, Mexico, Norway, the Philippines, Tunisia, Turkey and Honduras. Although no longer in front-line American service, the M1 is still in use by some National Guard units.

Above: *The .30 Rifle M1 (Garand).*

Browning Automatic Rifle — United States

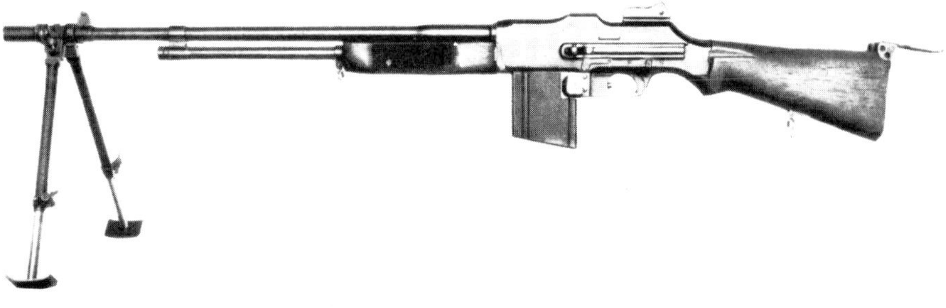

M1918A2
Calibre: .30in(7.62mm)
Length: 121.5cm
Length of Barrel: 61cm
Weight Empty: 8.82kg
Magazine Capacity: 20 rounds
Muzzle Velocity: 860m/s
Maximum Effective Range: 600m
Rate of Fire: 550rpm(cyclic)
350rpm(slow automatic)

The Browning Automatic Rifle, or BAR, can be regarded as either a heavy automatic rifle or a rather light LMG. Since its introduction into US Army service in 1918 it was used as a squad fire support weapon and remained in use with the Americans until well into the 1960's—the last production models were made during the Korean War. There were three main models of the BAR, the M1918, the M1918A1 and the M1918A2. The M1918 was

Above: *The Browning Automatic Rifle Model M1918A2.*

the basic hand-held model, the M1918A1 had a bipod and the M1918A2 retained the bipod and had two rates of automatic fire and no semi-automatic feature. Licence-built models were produced by FN in Belgium in the 1930's and others were made in Poland and Sweden. Some American police forces still use a commercial model, the 'Monitor', and the BAR is still in army use in Greece, Costa Rica, Guatemala, Indonesia, Mexico, Norway and the Philippines.

.30 M1903 Rifle Series — United States

M1903A1
Calibre: .30in(7.62mm)
Length: 109.7cm
Length of Barrel: 61cm
Weight: 3.95kg
Magazine Capacity: 5 rounds
Muzzle Velocity: 823m/s
Maximum Effective Range: 600m

Despite its age, the M1903 series of rifles (the M1903, M1903A1, M1903A3 and M1903A4) are still to be encountered in areas of American influence. Often known as the Springfield, the M1903 range remained in use throughout World War 2 and the M1903A3 continued to be produced until 1943. The M1903A4 was fitted with a telescopic sight. Although the M1903 has now been almost universally taken out of front line service, it is still used as a weapon by local militia and self-defence units in all parts of the world. The Mauser action used is sturdy and well made and the Springfield is likely to remain in use for years to come. The series is favoured for match shooting.

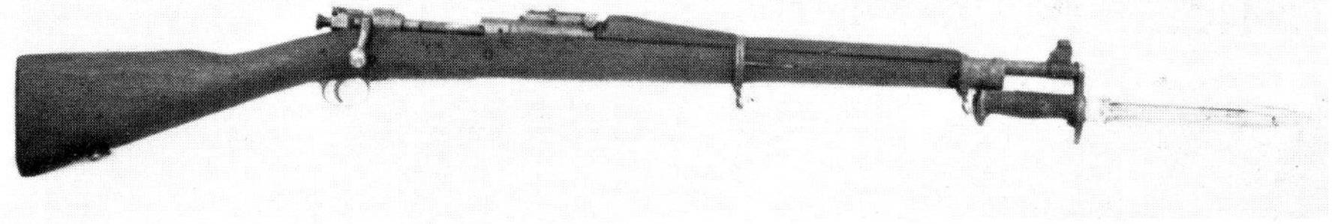

Below: *The .30 M1903 Rifle complete with bayonet.*

Special Purpose Individual Weapon — United States

Development of the SPIW started in the 1950's and a variety of prototypes have been built by a number of companies and government establishments. Among the companies have been Harrington and Richardson, Aircraft Armaments Incorporated and Olin-Winchester. To date none of the weapons have been placed in production. Currently a number of companies and establishments in the United States are working on a weapon to replace the current M16 rifle; the programme is known as the Future Rifle System.

Squad Automatic Weapon System — United States

The SAWS Programme is under way to find a replacement for the current M60 Machine Gun. Three companies have each built prototypes which fire a 6mm round. These are the XM233 (by the Maremont Corporation), the XM234 (by Aeronutronic-Ford) and the XM235 (by the Rodman Laboratories) In 1975 however the Department of Defense decided that the weapons must fire a 5.56mm round and it appears that only the XM235 can be modified to accept this. Other contenders in this programme are the Belgian Minimi machine gun, German HK21, Colt CMG-2 and the Maremont Universal Machine Gun.

The SAWS weapons all have bipods and an integral magazine and are capable of firing either single shots or bursts of full automatic.

Above: *The XM233 SAWS contender.*

Hughes 5.56mm Lockless Light Machine Gun

United States

Calibre: 5.56mm
Length: 109.2cm
Weight: 8.165kg(with magazine containing 200 rounds)
Magazine Capacity: 200 rounds
Range: 600m
Rate of Fire: 420 rounds per minute

The 5.56mm Lockless Light Machine Gun (LLMG) is an advanced automatic weapon which, coupled with its plastic cased ammunition, represents a major advance in the field of small arms. Sponsored initially by the Advanced Research Projects Agency and now under contract to the United States Army Armament Command, the Hughes developed weapon is based on the Lockless principle of a sliding sleeve mechanism. This eliminates the need for the primary sealing function normally provided by the standard metallic cartridge case, thus the use of lighter and more compact plastic cased ammunition is feasible and has been demonstrated.

The weapon is provided with a detachable bipod and is gas operated. The expendable magazine can be loaded and stored indefinitely and its capacity is six times that of any assault weapon and double that of all existing light machine guns.

The Hughes designed, plastic cased, fully telescoped rectangular cartridge uses a 5.56mm projectile weighing 68 grains, as compared with the standard 55 grains projectile. Test firings have already demonstrated both superior ballistics and an excellent growth potential. The round has a m/v of 914m/s. The weapon is still being developed and is not yet in production.

Below: *The Hughes 5.56mm Lockless Light Machine Gun.*

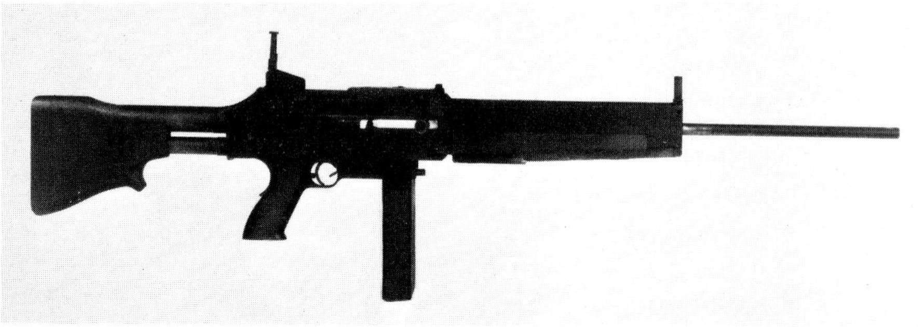

Lockless Rifle/Machine Gun

United States

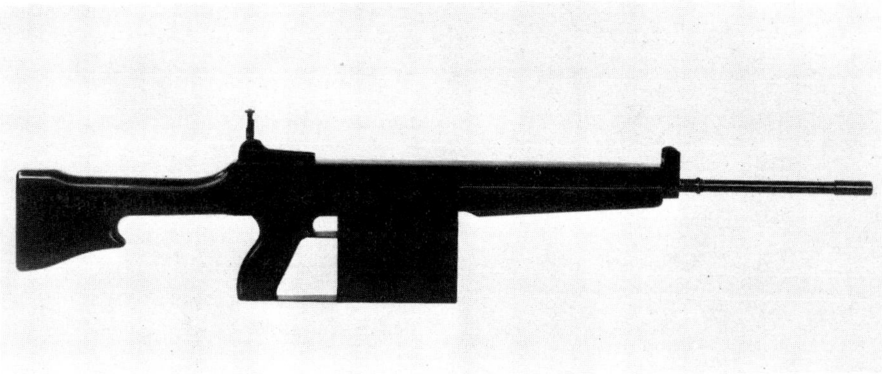

Calibre: 5.56mm
Length: 101.6cm(overall)
74.87cm(stock folded)
Length of Barrel: 55.8cm
Weight: 4.44kg(with magazine)
Magazine Capacity: 64 rounds
Muzzle Velocity: 944m/s
Effective Range: 600m
Rate of Fire: 420rpm

The Lockless Rifle/Machine Gun (LRMG) has been developed by the Ordnance Division of the Hughes Company of Culver City, California. The LRMG is the result of Hughes' continued work on a prototype funded under the Advanced Research Projects Agency. The weapon has a number of interesting features, and is based on the 'lockless' principle of a sliding sleeve mechanism.

It fires a new 5.56mm 68grain fully-telescoped rectangular cartridge with a case of plastic construction. The LRMG is gas-operated and the firer can select either single shots or full automatic fire. A detachable bipod is provided and the barrel can be quickly changed. According to Hughes it takes only three seconds to change the magazine.

Above: *The Hughes Lockless Rifle/Machine Gun.*

Colt 5.56mm CMG-2 Machine Gun

United States

Calibre: 5.56mm
Length: 106.5cm
Weight: 5.9kg(guns only)
7.31kg(complete with drum and bipod)
Range: 800m with 68grain bullet
600m with 55grain bullet
Muzzle Velocity: 991m/s, or 884m/s with 68 grain bullet
Rate of Fire: 650rpm(cyclic)
120rpm(sustained)

The Colt 5.56mm CMG-2 Machine Gun has been developed to the prototype stage by the Military Arms Division of Colt Industries who also make the current M16A1 Rifle. The weapon is at present under evaluation and has not yet been placed in production.

It is gas-operated and its method of locking is of the rotating bolt type. It is belt fed from a 150-round drum which is underneath the weapon and the barrel can be quickly changed. A carrying handle is provided over the barrel. The foresight is of the fixed post type and the rearsight is of the aperture type.

Although the CMG-2 can fire the standard 5.56mm 55grain M193 cartridge a more powerful cartridge with 68grains has been developed. This has a lower muzzle velocity but a longer range.

Note—the Colt CMG-1 5.56mm system which comprised a rifle, LMG gun MMG and an armoured vehicle MG, was not developed beyond the prototype stage.

Maremont 7.62mm Universal Machine Gun — United States

Calibre: 7.62mm
Length: 93.9cm(with butt stock and flash suppressor)
87.94cm(when used in fixed mount)
Weight: 6.8kg(without bipod)
Rate of Fire: 600 rounds per minute

This weapon has been developed by the Maremont Corporation, who currently build the M60 7.62mm machine gun. It has been designed for both ground and vehicle use and Maremont suggest that it could replace the 7.62mm M60 and the 7.62mm M73 (vehicle) machine guns. It is smaller and lighter than the M60 and simpler than the M73.

With a minimum interchangeability of parts, it can be either a recoil operated weapon for rigid enclosed mounting, or a gas operated weapon for infantry use, 85 per cent of the parts are basic to either type of weapon. As a possible special purpose weapon, it could be built to include both recoil and gas operated features with a simple selector system. The design is based on well known principles of operation, firing from the open bolt position using a rotary front locking bolt with three lugs. There is a quick change barrel and a reversible feed mechanism for right or left hand feed. The current design is chambered for the 7.62mm round, but other rounds could be used with little redesign. The Maremont 7.62mm Universal Machine Gun is a private venture by Maremont, and has no government backing at the present time.

Below: *The Maremont 7.62mm Universal Machine Gun without bipod.*

7.62mm M60 GPMG — United States

Calibre: 7.62mm
Length: 110cm
Length of Barrel: 56cm
Weight: 10.48kg
Type of Feed: link belt
Muzzle Velocity: 860m/s
Maximum Effective Range(Bipod): 800m
Maximum Effective Range(Tripod): 1800m
Rate of Fire: 550rpm(cyclic)
200rpm(automatic)

The concept of the General Purpose Machine Gun in the United States was accelerated during World War 2 by confrontation with the German MG34 and MG42. An American GPMG was designed along the lines of the MG42 in a series of guns in the series T44, T52 and T161. The T161 became the M60 and the design incorporates a modified MG42 feed with the operating mechanism of the German FG42. The prime producer of the M60 has been the Maremount Manufacturing Co of Saco in Maine, and large numbers have been produced to equip all arms of the US forces. Despite the protracted development of the M60 it still has some debatable features—the barrel heats quickly and is not easy to change rapidly, and the carrying handle is fragile and awkward. Also the M60 is rather on the heavy side for use as a squad weapon. Mounted on the M122 tripod, the M60 has limitations on sustained fire. Vehicle mounting is the M4 pedestal mount. Basically, the M60 is gas-operated and can fire automatic only. A bipod is fitted as standard and is also used for barrel-changing. As well as being the standard American GPMG, the M60 is also used by Australia and Taiwan, and was widely issued to many SE Asian countries.

The M60C and M60D are conversions of the basic M60 for use on helicopters.

Top right: *The standard M60 Machine Gun on a bipod.*

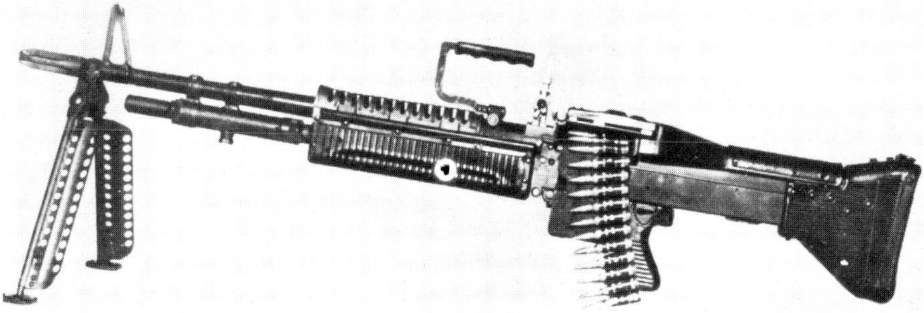

.30 Browning M1919A6 Machine Gun — United States

Calibre: .30in(7.62mm)
Length Overall: 134.6cm
Length of Barrel: 61cm
Weight Complete: 14.77kg
Type of Feed: 250-round belt
Muzzle Velocity: 860m/s
Maximum Effective Range: 1 000m
Rate of Fire: 400–550rpm(cyclic)
120rpm(automatic)

At the beginning of World War 2 the US Army found itself without an LMG and took steps to procure one by adapting the M1919A4. By the addition of a bipod, butt stock and pistol grip a rather heavy but serviceable light machine gun was produced and it was produced in some numbers as the M1919A6. After 1945, the M1919A6 was gradually withdrawn from use, despite a brief respite during the Korean War, and was sold or given to many friendly nations. Today, it would appear that its use is now confined to the armies of Taiwan, Turkey and Pakistan, but it is no doubt held as a reserve weapon by many other countries.

Below: *The .30 Browning M1919A6 Machine Gun.*

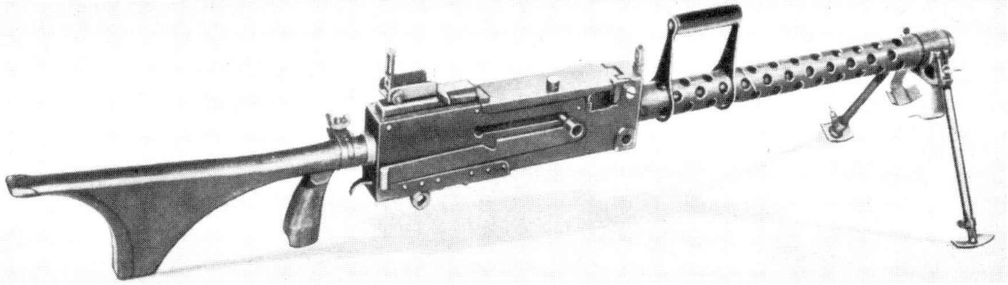

.30 Browning M1919A4 Machine Gun — United States

Calibre: .30in(7.62mm)
Length: 104.4cm
Length of Barrel: 61cm
Weight of Gun: 14.1kg
Weight of M2 Tripod: 6.36kg
Type of Feed: 250-round belt
Muzzle Velocity: 860m/s
Maximum Effective Range: 1 000m
Rate of Fire: 400–550rpm(cyclic)
120rpm(practical)

The M1919A4 is an air-cooled version of the earlier M1917 water-cooled machine gun which apparently is no longer in service anywhere. The M1919A4 was produced in large numbers during World War 2 and has proved itself to be a reliable weapon. As a result it is still likely to be found on a wide range of tripods, AA-mountings and vehicle and AFV pintles. One of the more common mountings is the Tripod M2. As well as remaining in widespread use with the US forces, the

M1919A4 is in service with the following countries:

Canada (rechambered for the NATO cartridge as the 7.62mm Machine Gun C1), Taiwan, Denmark (.30 M52-1), Dominica, Greece, Guatemala, Haiti, Israel, Iran, Italy, South Korea, Liberia, Mexico, Panama, Spain, Vietnam, Turkey.

Above: *The .30 Browning M1919A4 Machine Gun on a tripod.*

Browning .5 M2 Machine Gun

United States

M2HB
Calibre: .5in(12.7mm)
Length Overall: 165.3cm
Length of Barrel: 114.3cm
Weight: 37.8kg
Type of Feed: 110-round linked belts
Muzzle Velocity: 893m/s
Maximum Effective Range: 1 000m
Rate of Fire: 450–575rpm(cyclic)

The Browning family of .5 machine guns was initiated just after World War 1 and since then the basic mechanism and receiver has remained virtually unchanged. The type of barrel and cooling method have been changed from model to model but today the version most likely to be encountered is the M2HB (HB-heavy barrel). This version has an air-cooled barrel and it can be mounted on a variety of vehicle pintles or on the M3 tripod or M63 anti-aircraft mounting. The M2 is a powerful weapon that has not lost its place in modern armouries, despite its age. The round fired by the M2 is useful against light armour and low-flying aircraft and helicopters, and as an anti-personnel projectile it is almost unrivalled. However, the size and weight of the M2 mean that it is more likely to be used from a vehicle pintle than a ground mounting. More Browning .5 machine guns have been made than any other American machine gun.

Other users:
Argentina, Australia, Austria, Belgium, Canada, Chile, Denmark (m/50), France, Haiti, Iran, Israel, Italy, Japan, South Korea, Liberia, Morocco, Netherlands, Norway, Pakistan, Spain, Taiwan, Turkey.

Bottom left: *The .50 Browning Machine Gun.*

66mm Rocket M72A1 and M72A2 — United States

Calibre: 66mm
Length of Rocket: 50.8cm
Weight of Rocket: 1kg
Muzzle Velocity: 145m/s
Maximum Effective Range: 300m
Armour Penetration: 305mm steel plate
Length of Launcher Closed: 65.5cm
Length of Launcher Extended: 89.3cm
Weight Complete: 2.37kg

Designed as a one-man rocket launcher for anti-tank use, the M72 has been replaced in service by the M72A1 and M72A2 (the two are identical except that the M72A2 has an increased penetration capability). When carried, the smooth-bore launcher tube is carried closed, and in this form is water-proof. In action, the end covers are opened, which is done by removing safety pins, and the inner tube is telescope outwards and this cocks the firing mechanism. The launcher tube is then held over the shoulder, aimed by the simple sights and fired by pressing the trigger button. The rocket motor is fully burnt by the time it leaves the launcher but this also leaves a large 'danger' area behind the firer. Once used, the launcher tube is discarded. The 66mm rocket has now become a standard infantry anti-tank weapon in many armies. The M71A1 and M71A2 are 35mm sub-calibre training devices. The model is also built in Norway by Raufoss for issue to NATO forces.

Below: *The 66mm M72 Anti-Tank Rocket.*

90mm Recoilless Rifle M67

United States

Calibre: 90mm
Length: 134.6cm
Weight: 15.876kg
Range: 450m
Crew: 1–2

The M67 is an air-cooled portable anti-tank weapon and can be fired from the prone position or the shoulder. It is being replaced in the United States Army by the Dragon ATGW.

It consists of a front mounting bracket group, cable assembly, face shield group, breech and hinge mechanism group, rear mounting bracket group and the rifled tube itself. It is fitted with a M103 telescope which was a magnification of × 3 and a 10° field of view.

It fires a fin-stabilised HEAT round weighing 3.1kg which has a m/v of 213m/s. An anti-personnel round has also been developed.

Below: *The 90mm Recoilless Rifle M67.*

57mm M18 Recoilless Rifle

United States

Calibre: 57mm
Length: 156.2cm
Length of Barrel: 122cm
Weight: 18.2kg
Range: 400m(effective)
4 000m(maximum)
Crew: 1–2

There are three basic models of this weapon, the M18, M18A1 and the T15E16. These can be fired from the ground, shoulder or from a M74 or M1917A2 mount. The complete weapon consists of the barrel group, breech mechanism group, a firing cable group, trigger mechanism group, bipod assembly and an extendable nandle assembly.

The M18 and M18A1 have their chamber and breechblock handles located in different positions. The M18 has its on the left and the M18A1 is on the right. The major differences between the M18A1 and the T15E16 is in the linkage between the trigger mechanism group and the breech mechanism group. The following types of ammunition are available: HE (m/v 365m/s), HEAT (m/v 365m/s), canister, WP (m/v 365m/s) and TP. Its effective range in the anti-tank role is approx 400m and its maximum range, at 39° elevation, with a HEAT round is 4 000m. It is provided with an M86F (M86C) telescope which has a 7° field of view and a magnification of 2.8.

The M18 is built in Communist China under the designation of Type 36.

Above: *A 57mm M18 recoilless rifle being used by the Norwegian Army.*

3.5inch Rocket Launcher M20 — United States

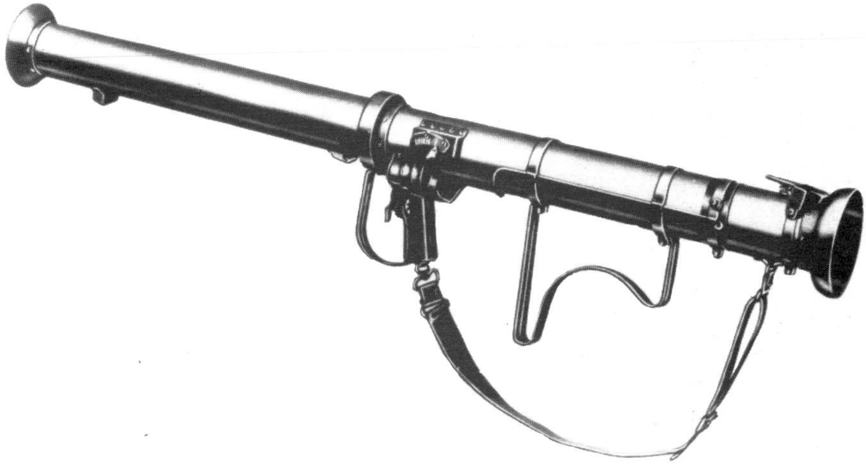

Calibre: 3.5in(88.9mm)
Weight of Rocket: 4.04kg
Weight of Rocket Warhead: 0.87kg
Length of Launcher: 154.9cm
Weight: 5.5kg
Muzzle Velocity: 97 to 147m/s
Maximum Effective Range(A/T): 110m
Maximum Range: 1 200m
Rate of Fire: 6 shots per min.

The M20 was developed from the earlier 2.36in M9A1 rocket launcher at the time of the Korean War and since that time it has kept its place as one of the main anti-tank weapons of many armies. The M20, often known as the 'Bazooka', is a simple rocket launcher firing a hollow-charge rocket projectile to relatively short ranges. It requires a two-man team. When carried, the long tube is folded into two for easier handling. In action a rocket is loaded into the open breech and two wires are secured to two electrical terminals. When the trigger is pulled a small electrical current ignites the rocket motor which projects the rocket forward, leaving a large and dangerous flame area behind the projector. Although the M20 and its developments the M20A1, M20A1B1 and M20AB2, are no longer in front-line service with the US forces, they remain in use with many other armies but they are gradually being replaced. China continues to use a copy known as the Type 51, and many

Above: *The 3.5inch Rocket Launcher M20.*

smaller countries make their own ammunition, Spain (the firm of Instalaza SA) being an example.

Other Users:
Argentina, China, Denmark(89 mm RK M/51), Dominica, France(LRAC M20), Greece, Guatemala, India, Iran, Italy, Japan, South Korea, Liberia, Malaysia, Morocco, Norway, Pakistan, Panama, Portugal, Spain(88.9mm Model 65 Lanzagranadas), Turkey, Vietnam.

40mm Grenade Launcher M79 — United States

Calibre: 40mm
Weight of Grenade: 0.227kg
Length: 73.7cm
Length of Barrel: 35.6cm
Weight Empty: 2.72kg
Weight Loaded: 2.95kg
Muzzle Velocity: 76m/s
Maximum Range: 400m(approx)
Maximum Effective Range: 150m(point targets)

The M79 is a break-open single-shot weapon designed to be fired from the shoulder. It is breech-loaded and fires a 40mm metal cartridge case with an internal primer. The ammunition available covers a wide range from smoke to HE and riot rounds, and these rounds can be fired to a range in excess of that obtainable by normal rifle grenades with a reasonable degree of accuracy. The rear sights on the M79 are near the muzzle as the low m/v requires high elevation angles to reach maximum ranges. Although it is still in widespread use with the American forces, the M79 is gradually being replaced by the smaller and lighter M203 launcher which can be fitted onto the M16 rifle.

Below: *The 40mm Grenade Launcher M79.*

40mm Automatic Grenade Launcher XM174 — United States

Calibre: 40mm
Weight of Grenade: 0.227kg
Length: 71.12cm
Weight Loaded(Less Pintle): 11.75kg
Magazine Capacity: 12 rounds
Muzzle Velocity(Normal Rounds): 76m/s
Maximum Range(Normal Rounds): 400m
Maximum Range(New Rounds): 1 000m

The success of the M79 grenade launcher has led to the normal infantry squad having a greatly increased fire power against area targets. Since the M79 and the M203 are both only single-shot weapons, a demand for an automatic launcher arose. The result is the XM174 Automatic Grenade Launcher, produced by the Aerojet Ordnance and Manufacturing Co of Downey, California. This weapon uses a conventional blow-back mechanism which can be selected for automatic or semi-automatic fire, and grenades are held in a twelve-round magazine on the LHS of the receiver. The XM174 is designed primarily for use from vehicles, fitted on a pintle, but it can also be fitted to the M122 tripod. At present the range of the XM174

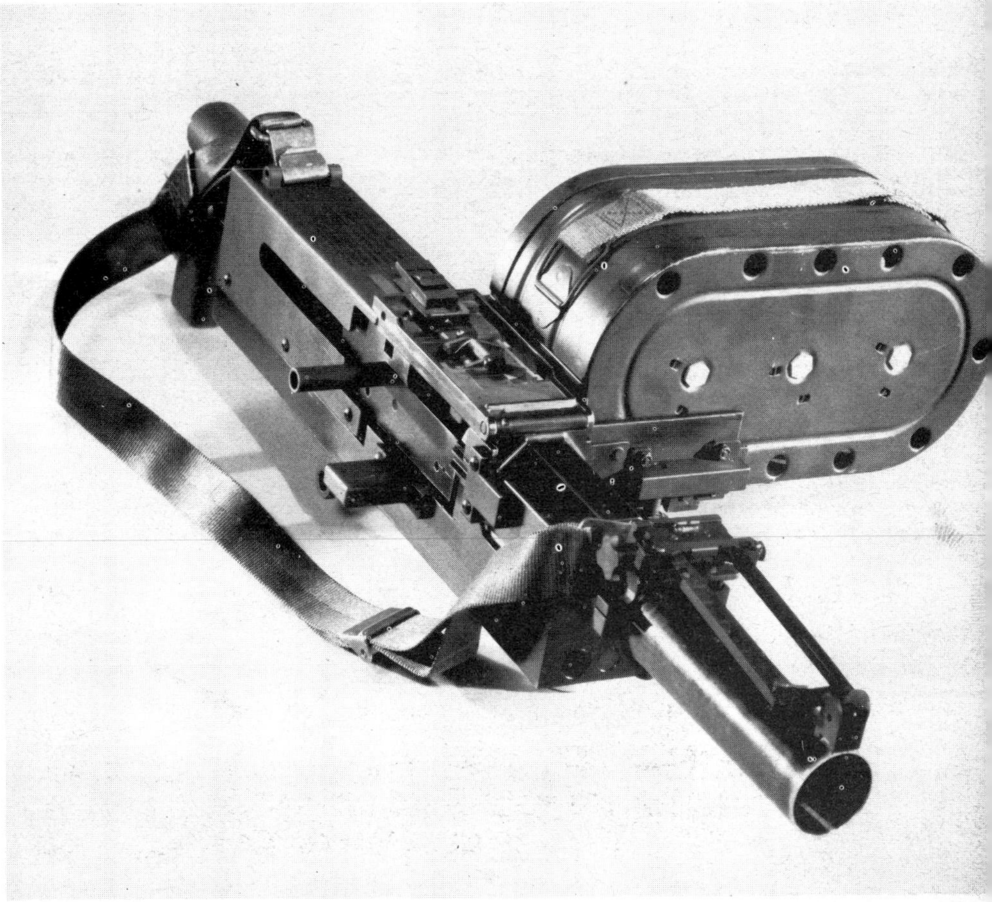

is limited by the current grenades in service but a new series of grenades is under development which will have a range of up to 1 000 metres. At the time of writing the latest version is the XM174E3 under extended trials by the US Marine Corps.

Above: *The 40mm Automatic Grenade Launcher XM174 without tripod.*

60mm XM224 Mortar

United States

Development of the 60mm XM224 mortar commenced in December 1970 as a replacement for both the 60mm M19 and 81mm M29 mortars. Development has now been completed and it is expected to enter service in the near future. It will probably be deployed with Airborne, Airmobile and Marine units where its light weight will be an advantage.

The circular baseplate is an aluminium forging and a lightweight rectangular baseplate has also been developed. Total weight of the XM224, ie baseplate, barrel, bipod and sight is only 20.4kg.

The XM224 can be fired by the conventional gravity method or by a firing pin. The sight used is the XM64, this weighs 1.1kg.

The mortar bomb is provided with a multi-option fuse, this allows the crew to choose airburst, near-surface burst, direct action or delayed action.

A new lightweight laser rangefinder known as the AN/GVS-5 has been developed for use with the XM224. This weighs 2kg and can range up to 10 000m with an accuracy of ± 10m.

Left: *The 60mm XM224 Mortar.*

60mm Mortar M19

United States

Calibre: 60mm
Weight of Bomb(M49A2): 1.363kg
Length Overall: 81.9cm
Weight Complete: 20.545kg
Elevation(M5Mount): + 40° to + 85°
Maximum Range(M49A2): 1 790m
Rate of Fire: 30rpm(maximum)
18rpm(sustained)

The M19 was originally issued with a simple base plate, the M1, and no tripod. With the demise of the earlier 60mm Mortar M2, however, the M19 was fitted with the M5 tripod and remained in use for some years. It has now been largely replaced in front-line service with the American forces but it is still in widespread use in SE Asia and in many South American countries as is the earlier M2. China uses a copy of the M2 in the Type 31.

Below: *The 60mm M19 Light Mortar.*

M67 7.65mm Pistol

Yugoslavia

Calibre: 7.65mm
Length: 16.5cm
Length of Barrel: 9.4cm
Weight: .78kg(loaded)
.7kg(empty)
Magazine Capacity: 6 rounds
Range: 50m

This is one of the more recent Yugoslav pistols and has been manufactured in both 9mm and 7.65mm calibres. The 9mm weapon fires the 9 × 17mm cartridge whilst the 7.65mm weapon fires the 7.65mm × 17SR cartridge. It is believed that these weapons are in service with the Yugoslav Army. The Yugoslavs also build the Soviet TT-33 Pistol, this being known as the M-57. Other sources state that the TT-33 is known as the M54 (7.65mm) and M65 (9mm).

7.62mm Sub-Machine Gun M56 — Yugoslavia

Calibre: 7.62mm
Length: 104cm(with bayonet)
86.5cm(stock extended)
64cm(stock folded)
Length of Barrel: 25cm
Weight: 3.73kg(with loaded magazine)
3.38kg(with empty magazine)
3.06kg(without magazine)
Magazine Capacity: 32 rounds
Range: 200m(semi-automatic)
100m(automatic)
Rate of Fire: 570/620rpm(cyclic)
180rpm(automatic)
30rpm(semi-automatic)

The M56 was developed to replace the earlier M49 sub-machine gun. In appearance the M56 is similar to both the Soviet PPS M1943 SMG and the German MP-40. The M56 is blowback operated and is capable of both full automatic and semi-automatic fire. The M56 fires the same 7.62mm × 25 cartridge with a m/v of 500m/s as the earlier M49. It is provided with a folding stock and a bayonet can be fitted if required. The front sight is of the hooded post type and the rear sight is of the flip type set for 100 and 200m.

Above: *The 7.62mm M56 Sub-Machine Gun.*

7.62mm M49 Sub-Machine Gun — Yugoslavia

Calibre: 7.62mm
Length: 87.4cm
Length of Barrel: 27.3cm
Weight: 4.66kg(with loaded magazine
4.25kg(with empty magazine)
3.96kg(without magazine)
Magazine Capacity: 35 rounds
Range: 200m(semi-automatic)
100m(automatic)
Rate of Fire: 700rpm(cyclic)
120/150rpm(automatic)
30/40rpm(semi-automatic)

The M49 is a Yugoslav weapon developed from the Soviet PPSh-41 which was used in large numbers by Yugoslavia. The main differences lay in the bolt, buffer assembly and the barrel casing. The M49 has circular holes in the casing rather than the long slots which are found on the Soviet weapon. Also, the Yugoslav weapon has only a 35-round magazine although it will accept a Soviet PPSh-41 magazine. The M49 is blowback operated and can be used either full automatic or semi-automatic. Its front sight is of the blade post type and its rearsights are of the flip type graduated for 100 and 200m. It fires the 7.62mm × 25 cartridge with a m/v of 500m/s or the 7.63mm Mauser cartridge.

7.62mm M64A Assault Rifle (or Model 70) — Yugoslavia

Calibre: 7.62mm
Length: 115.7cm(with bayonet)
95.7cm
Length of Barrel: 41.5cm
Weight: 4.19kg(with loaded aluminium magazine)
4.25kg(with loaded late steel magazine)
4.35kg(with loaded early steel magazine)
3.69kg(with empty aluminium magazine)
3.75kg(with empty late steel magazine)
3.85kg(with empty early steel magazine)
3.46kg(without magazine)
Magazine Capacity: 20 or 30 rounds
Range: 400m
Rate of Fire: 600rpm(cyclic)
40/120rpm(practical)

There are three models of this weapon built in Yugoslavia. The first of these is the M64 which has a barrel 100mm longer than that of the M64A, this is therefore referred to as an automatic rifle rather than an assault rifle. All are based on the Soviet AK assault rifle. The second model is the M64A which more recently has become known as the Model 70 assault rifle; this has a fixed wooden stock. The third model is the M64B which recently has become known as the Model 70A; this has a folding stock. These weapons have a permanently attached spigot type grenade launcher. When the grenade sight is raised it cuts off the supply to the gas cylinder.

Bottom left and above: *The Yugoslav 7.62mm M64B (Or Model 70A) Assault Rifle. This has a folding stock, grenade launching sight and a compensator screwed onto the barrel.*

7.62mm Rifle M59/66

Yugoslavia

Calibre: 7.62mm
Length: 132cm(with bayonet)
125.5cm
Length of Barrel: 52cm
Weight: 4.2kg(loaded)
4.03kg(with empty magazine)
Magazine Capacity: 10 rounds
Range: 400m
Rate of Fire: 30rpm

The first M59 was a direct copy of the Soviet SKS (Simonov) rifle. The M59/66 was a later development by the Yugoslavs. The main differences are that it has a longer knife type bayonet and a permanently attached spigot type grenade launcher. When the grenade sight is not required it is folded flat behind the foresight. The M59/66 fires the 7.62mm × 39 cartridge with a m/v of 735m/s. The M59/66 can fire the following types of rifle grenades, as can the M48 rifle:
F-1/N60: Weight .632kg, range 240m.
PGN 60: Weight .58kg, range 100m(anti-tank).
YugAT: Weight .602kg, range 150m(anti-tank).
YugAPers: Weight .52kg, range 400m(anti-personnel).

7.62mm M65A Light Machine Gun — Yugoslavia

Calibre: 7.62mm
Length: 109.5cm
Length of Barrel: 47cm
Weight: 5.45kg
Magazine Capacity: 30 rounds
Range: 600m
Rate of Fire: 600rpm(cyclic)
120rpm(automatic-M65B)
80rpm(automatic-M65A)
40rpm(semi-automatic)

This weapon is based on the Yugoslav assault rifle M64A which in turn is based on the Soviet AK weapon. The M65A has a fixed barrel whilst the M65B has a quick-change barrel. Both weapons are gas-operated with a selective fire facility, and fire the 7.62mm × 39 cartridge with a m/v of 732m/s. The foresight is of the cylindrical post type and the rearsight is of the leaf notch type. Yugoslavia also uses the German World War 2 MG42 (qv) machine gun which they call the M53 SARAC.

Anti-Tank Grenade Launcher RB-57 — Yugoslavia

Calibre: 90mm(launcher)
44mm(tube)
Weight of Launcher: 8.35kg
Length of Tube: 96cm
Range: 1 200m(maximum)
400m(effective stationary targets)
200m(effective moving targets)
Rate of Fire: 4rpm
Crew: 2 men

After the World War 2 the Yugoslavs developed a number of anti-tank launchers. The first model was called the M49 (or RB-49) and fired a HEAT round. It was provided with a folding bipod, shoulder rest and sling but did not go into service. One unusual feature of the M49 was that it had a six-round magazine for ignition cartridges.

The current Yugoslav anti-tank grenade launcher is the M57 (or RB-57) as it is often called. Late models are known as the M57A (or RB-57A) and M57A2 (or RB-57A2). Each fires a HEAT round weighing 2.44kg and 1.104m in length, m/v is 145m/s, the projectile itself is 75.7cm in length and weighs 1.84kg. It will penetrate 270mm of armour.

The M57 is provided with conventional sights for 100, 200, 300 and 400m; in addition there is an emergency sight for 200m. An optical sight is also available, sighted to 400m. The sight is on the LHS with the loader to the right. A bipod is provided.

The primers for the projectile are located in the sidewall of the tailboom with a right angle flash channel leading to the propellent. The spring loaded striker, which is at the bottom of the launcher tube, is actuated by a double action trigger mechanism.

Below: *The RB-57 Anti-Tank Grenade Launcher.*

60mm M57 Light Mortar

Yugoslavia

Calibre: 60.75mm
Total Weight: 19.7kg
5.5kg(barrel)
4.5kg(bipod)
8.85kg(baseplate)
Length of Barrel: 70.8cm
Elevation: +45° to +83°
Traverse: 7°
Range: 1690m(maximum)
74m(minimum)
Rate of Fire: 25–30rpm(maximum)
Crew: 2

Essentially a Yugoslav model of the American 60mm mortar M2, the M57 fires a bomb weighing 1.35kg at a m/v of 159m/s. Types of bomb available include HE, smoke and illuminating. The crew normally consists of two men, the aimer on the left and the loader on the right.

The Yugoslavs also have a 50mm light mortar called the M8 which is similar to the British 2in mortar. Basic data is as follows: calibre 50mm, weight 7.3kg, weight of bomb .92kg, maximum range 480m and minimum range 135m.

Bibliography

There are many excellent publications on small arms, listed below are the standard reference books on the subject. Without doubt *Jane's Infantry Weapons* is the most authoritative book on infantry weapons. The first edition was edited by the late Major F. W. A. Hobart, one of the world's leading experts of small arms design and development. Other publications include:

Book of Pistols by W. H. B. Smith and J. E. Smith (Arms and Armour Press, London)
Book of Rifles by W. H. B. Smith and J. E. Smith (Arms and Armour Press, London)
Jane's Infantry Weapons, 1975 by Major F. W. A. Hobart (Macdonald Jane's of London)
Jane's Infantry Weapons, 1976 by D. H. Archer (Macdonald Jane's of London)
Leichte Infanteriewaffen by Nikolaus Krivinyi (Verlag Carl Uebereuter, Vienna)
Military Small Arms of the 20th Century by I. Hogg and John Weeks (Arms and Armour Press, London)
Pictorial History of the Machine Gun by Major F. W. A. Hobart (Ian Allan, London)
Pictorial History of the Rifle by G. W. P. Swenson (Ian Allan, London)
Pictorial History of the Sub-Machine Gun by Major F. W. A. Hobart (Ian Allan, London)
Small Arms of the World (Arms and Armour Press, London)

Photo Credits

The photographs used to illustrate this book have been received from many governments, companies and individuals all over the world. Special thanks are due to the staff of the Pattern Room at The Royal Small Arms Factory at Enfield Lock, Middlesex, for their assistance in taking some of the photographs used in this book. The sources of photographs, where known, are listed below:–

Aerojet Ordnance and Manufacturing Company (USA) 131
Argentine Ministry of Defence 8(T)
Armalite Incorporated 113(C & B)
Austrian Army 10(B), 11, 51(B)
Beretta of Italy 71, 72, 73, 74, 75
Breda (Italy) 76
Carl Walther (Germany) 43, 45(B), 46(T)
Colt Industries (USA) 115
Esperanza Company (Spain) 97, 98
FFV (Sweden) 101, 102, 103
Finnish Army 30, 31, 32
FN of Herstal (Belgium) 12, 14(T), 15, 16, 17
French Army (ECPA) 33, 34, 35, 36, 37, 38, 39
German Army 42(B)
Heckler and Koch (Germany) 44(B), 45(T), 47, 48, 49(T & C), 51(T)
Hughes Helicopters and Ordnance Systems (USA) 122(B), 123
Interdynamics Company (Sweden) 100 (T & C)
Irish Army 99
Israel Military Industrial 68, 69, 71(T)
Maremont Corporation (USA) 122(T), 124, 125(T)
MBB (Germany) 54
Ministry of Defence Army (CCR) 62, 116
Norwegian Army 129(T)
Peter Chamberlain 58(B), 60, 63
Rheinmetall Company (Germany) 52
Soltam Company (Israel) 70(B)
Sterling Armament Company (Britain) 56, 57(T & C)
Sturm Ruger and Company (USA) 113(T)
Swiss Industrial Group 104, 105, 106, 108
Terry Gander 8(B), 9(T), 13, 14(B), 18, 20, 21, 22, 23, 24, 25, 26, 27, 28, 29, 44(T), 46(B), 49(B), 50, 53, 55, 57(B), 58(T), 59, 61, 64(T), 66, 67, 78, 79, 80, 81, 83, 85, 86, 88, 89, 90, 91, 92, 93(T), 94, 95, 96, 100(F), 107, 110, 111, 112, 114, 117, 118(T), 119, 120, 121, 125(B), 126, 127, 130, 134, 135, 136
Thomson-Brandt 39, 40, 41, 42(T)
United Kingdom Land Forces 64(B), 65
United States Army 1, 2, 3, 128, 129(B), 132, 133
United States Marine Corps 118(B)
Voer Company (Austria) 9(B), 10(T)

Index